An Inspirational
TREASURY
of
SAMUEL
RUTHERFORD

An Inspirational Treasury of Samuel Rutherford
© Copyright 2001 Stanley Barnes

ISBN 1 84030 102 3

Ambassador Publications
a division of
Ambassador Productions Ltd.
Providence House
Ardenlee Street,
Belfast,
BT6 8QJ
Northern Ireland
www.ambassador-productions.com

Emerald House
427 Wade Hampton Blvd.
Greenville
SC 29609, USA
www.emeraldhouse.com

An Inspirational

TREASURY
of
SAMUEL
RUTHERFORD

❖ AN APPRECIATION OF RUTHERFORD
❖ SELECTED SAYINGS
❖ LIVING INSIGHTS AND ILLUSTRATIONS
❖ THE SERAPHIC LETTERS
❖ THE SANDS OF TIME ARE SINKING
❖ QUAINT SERMONS OF RUTHERFORD

Compiled & Written by
Stanley Barnes

AMBASSADOR
BELFAST, NORTHERN IRELAND
GREENVILLE, USA

CONTENTS

INTRODUCTION

The dawn of a new millennium marked the 400th anniversary of the birth of Samuel Rutherford. Although regarded as a brilliant scholar, contender for the faith and a learned theologian, he is best remembered today for his *Seraphic Letters*. Rutherford could say, like the ancient prophet Jeremiah, "I am the man that hath seen affliction." He suffered the affliction of losing his first wife, and eight of his nine children predeceasing him; the affliction of being cast out of his charge at Anwoth and exiled to Aberdeen; the affliction of standing alone when former friends weakened their stance in the cause of Christ's crown and covenant. Nevertheless the university of adversity taught him to recline upon the bosom of his Beloved as did John the beloved disciple. In his letters he exhorts the afflicted to do the same when he says,

> "There are many heads lying in Christ's bosom and there
> is room for yours among the rest. Go where ye will,
> your soul shall not sleep sound but in Christ's bosom."

The spiritual counsel and encouragements that can be gleaned from this Treasury are just as needful and relevant in our day as they were in Rutherford's.

The Saint of the Covenant has left the Church a rich legacy in his letters and writings that feeds both the soul and the mind.

The aim of this Inspirational Treasury may be summed up in the words of Richard of Chichester's famous prayer – "That we may be enabled to know Jesus Christ more clearly, to love Him more dearly and to follow Him more nearly."

Stanley Barnes
September 2001.

Chapter One

AN APPRECIATION OF SAMUEL RUTHERFORD

∞

By Dr. Alexander Whyte

∞

Dr. Alexander Whyte rose from the depths of obscurity to the heights of popularity becoming one of Scotland's most distinguished pulpiteers and authors. He succeeded the famous Robert S. Candlish as minister of St. George's Free Church, Edinburgh and for nearly forty years he occupied that renowned pulpit. He loved to share with his congregation and especially the youth, great lessons and truths from the lives of godly men and women of past generations. When evangelists J. Wilbur Chapman and Charles Alexander came to Edinburgh for a campaign, Chapman took suddenly ill and Whyte was called upon to fill the pulpit. Not only was he a great preacher, but he was also a prolific author and some of his writings include; *A Commentary on the Shorter Catechism; Bunyan Characters; Character of Jesus Christ our Lord; The Apostle Paul; With Mercy and With Judgement; and Samuel Rutherford and Some of His Correspondents.*

This abridged appreciation of the Life of Samuel Rutherford is taken from his 'Thirteen Appreciations' published in Edinburgh and London by Oliphant, Anderson and Ferrier.

∞

SAMUEL RUTHERFORD, the author of the seraphic *Letters,* was born in the south of Scotland in the year of our Lord 1600. Thomas Goodwin was born in England the same year, Robert Leighton in 1611, Richard Baxter in 1615, John Owen in 1616, John Bunyan in 1628, and John Howe in 1630.

A little vellum-covered volume now lies open before me, the title-page of which runs thus: 'Joshua Redivivus, or Mr. Rutherford's Letters, now published for the use of the people of God: but more particularly for those who now are, or may afterwards be, put to suffering for Christ and His cause. By a wellwisher to the work and to the people of God. Printed in the year 1664.' That is all. It would not have been safe in 1664 to say more. There is no editor's name on the title page, no publisher's name, and no place of printing or of publication; only two texts of forewarning and reassuring Scripture, and then the year of grace 1664.

Joshua Redivivus: That is to say, Moses' spy and pioneer, Moses' successor and the captain of the Lord's covenanted host come back again. A second Joshua sent to Scotland to go before God's people in that land and in that day; a spy who would both by his experience and by his testimony cheer and encourage the suffering people of God. For all this Samuel Rutherford truly was. As he said of himself in one of his letters to Hugh Mackail, he was indeed a spy sent out to make experiment upon the life of silence and separation, banishment and martyrdom, and to bring back a report of that life for the vindication of Christ and for the support and encouragement of His people. It was a happy thought of Rutherford's first editor, Robert McWard, his old Westminster Assembly secretary, to put at the top of his title-page, Joshua risen again from the dead, or, Mr. Rutherford's Letters written from his place of banishment in Aberdeen.

In selecting his twelve spies Moses went on the principle of choosing the best and the ablest men he could lay hold of in all Israel. And in selecting Samuel Rutherford to be the first sufferer for His covenanted people in Scotland, our Lord took a man who was already famous for his character and his services. For no man of his age in broad Scotland stood higher as a scholar, a theologian, a controversialist, a preacher and a very saint than Samuel Rutherford. He had been settled at Anwoth on the Solway in 1627, and for the next nine years he had lived such a noble life among his people as to make Anwoth famous as long as Jesus Christ has a Church in Scotland. As we say Bunyan and Bedford, Baxter and Kidderminster, Newton and Olney, Edwards and Northampton, Boston and Ettrick, McCheyne and Dundee, so we say Rutherford and Anwoth.

His talents, his industry, his scholarship, his preaching power, his pastoral solicitude and his saintly character all combined to make Rutherford a marked man both to the friends and to the enemies of the truth. His talents and his industry while he was yet a student in Edinburgh had carried him to the top of his classes, and all his days he could write in Latin better than either in Scotch or English. His habits of work at Anwoth soon became a very proverb. His people boasted that their minister was always at his books, always among his parishioners, always at their sick beds and their death-beds, always catechising their children, and always alone with his God. And then the matchless preaching at the parish church of Anwoth. We can gather what made the Sabbaths of Anwoth so memorable both to Rutherford and to his people from the books we still have from those great Sabbaths: *The Trial and the Triumph of Faith; Christ Dying and Drawing Sinners to Himself;* and suchlike masterly discourses. Rutherford was the 'most moving and the most affectionate of preachers,' a preacher determined to know nothing but Jesus Christ and Him crucified, but not so much crucified, as crucified and risen again - crucified indeed, but now glorified. Rutherford's life for his people at Anwoth had something altogether superhuman and unearthly about it. His correspondents in his own day and his critics in our day stumble at his too intense devotion to his charge; he lived for his congregation, they tell us, almost to the neglect of his wife and children. But by the time of his banishment his home was desolate, his wife and children were in the grave. And all the time and thought and love they had got from him while they were alive had, now that they were dead, returned with new and intensified devotion to his people and his parish.

> Fair Anwoth by the Solway,
> To me thou still art dear,
> E'en from the verge of heaven
> I drop for thee a tear.
> O! if one soul from Anwoth
> Meet me at God's right hand,
> My heaven will be two heavens
> In Immanuel's Land.

This, then, was the spy chosen by Jesus Christ to go out, first of all the ministers of Scotland, into the life of banishment in that day, so as to try its fords and taste its vineyards, and to report to God's straitened and persecuted people at home.

To begin with, it must always be remembered that Rutherford was not laid in irons in Aberdeen, or cast into a dungeon. He was simply deprived of his pulpit and of his liberty to preach, and was sentenced to live in silence in the town of Aberdeen. Like Dante, another great spy of God's providence and grace, Rutherford was less a prisoner than an exile. But if any man thinks that simply to be an exile is a small punishment, or a light cross, let him read the psalms and prophecies of Babylon, the *Divine Comedy,* and Rutherford's *Letters*

Yes, banishment was banishment; exile was exile; silent Sabbaths were silent Sabbaths; and a borrowed fireside with all its willing heat was still a borrowed fireside; and, in spite of all that the best people of Aberdeen could do for Samuel Rutherford, he felt the friendliest stairs of that city to be very steep to his feet, and its best bread to be very salt in his mouth.

But, with all that, Samuel Rutherford would have been but a blind and unprofitable spy for the best people of God in Scotland, for Marion McNaught, and Lady Kenmure, and Lady Culross, for the Cardonesses, father, mother and son, and for Hugh Mackail and such like, if he had tasted nothing more bitter than borrowed bread in

Aberdeen, and climbed nothing steeper than a granite stair. 'Paul had need,' Rutherford writes to Lady Kenmure, 'of the devil's service to buffet him, and far more, you and I.' I am downright afraid to tell you how Satan was sent to buffet Samuel Rutherford in his banishment, and how he was sifted as wheat is sifted in his exile. I would not expose such a saint of God to every eye, but I look for readers who know something of the plague of their own hearts, and who are comforted in their banishment and battle by nothing more than when they are assured that they are not alone in the deep darkness. 'When Christian had travelled in this disconsolate condition for some time he thought he heard the voice of a man as going before him and saying, "*Though I walk through the Valley of the Shadow of Death I will fear no ill, for Thou art with me.*" Then he was glad, and that for these reasons: - Firstly, because he gathered from thence that some one who feared God was in this valley as well as himself. Secondly, for that he perceived that God was with them though in that dark and dismal state; and why not, thought he, with me? Thirdly, for that he hoped, could he overtake them, to have company by and by.' And in like manner I am certain that it will encourage and save from despair some who now read this if I just report to them some of the discoveries and experiences of himself that Samuel Rutherford made among the siftings and buffetings of his Aberdeen exile. Writing to Lady Culross, he says: 'O my guiltiness, the follies of my youth and the neglects of my calling, they all do stare me in the face here; the world hath sadly mistaken me: no man knoweth what guiltiness is in me.' And to Lady Boyd, speaking of some great lessons he had learnt in the school of adversity, he says: 'In the third place, I have seen here my abominable vileness, and it is such that if I were well known no one in all the kingdom would ask me how I do.... I am a deeper hypocrite and a shallower professor than anyone could believe. Madam, pity me, the chief of sinners.' And again, to the Laird of Carlton: 'Woe, woe is me, that men should think there is anything in me. The house-devils that keep me company and this sink of corruption make me to carry low sails...But, howbeit I am a wretched captive of sin, yet my Lord can hew heaven out of worse timber than I am, if worse there be:' And to Lady Kenmure: 'I am somebody in the books of my friends, ...but there are armies of thoughts within me, saying the contrary, and laughing at the mistakes of my many friends. Oh! if my inner side were only seen!' Ah, no! My brethren, no land is so fearful to them that are sent to search it out as their own heart. 'The land,' said the ten spies, 'is a land that eateth up the inhabitants thereof; the cities are walled up to heaven, and very great, and the children of Anak dwell in them. We were, in their sight, as grasshoppers, and so we were in our own sight.' Ah, no! No stair is so steep as the stair of sanctification; no bread is so salt as that which is baked for a man of God out of the wild oats of his past sin and his present sinfulness. Even Joshua and Caleb, who brought back a good report of the land, did not deny that the children of Anak were there, or that their walls went up to heaven, or that they, the spies, were as grasshoppers before their foes: Caleb and Joshua only said that, in spite of all that, if the Lord delighted in His people, He both could and would give them a land flowing with milk and honey. And be it recorded and remembered to his credit and his praise that, with all his self-discoveries and self-accusings, Rutherford did not utter one single word of doubt or despair; so far from that was he, that in one of his letters to Hugh Mackail he tells us that some of his correspondents have written to him that he is possibly too joyful under the cross. Blunt old Knockbrex, for one, wrote to his old minister to restrain somewhat his ecstasy. So true was it, what Rutherford said of himself to David Dickson that he was 'made up of extremes.' So he was, for I know no man among all my masters in personal religion who unites greater extremes in himself than Samuel Rutherford. Who weeps like Rutherford over his banishment from Anwoth, while all the time who is so feasted in Christ's palace in Aberdeen? Who loathes himself like Rutherford? Not Bunyan, not Brodie, not Brea, not Boston; and, at the same time, who is so transported and lost to himself in the beauty and sweetness of Christ? As we read his raptures we almost say with cautious old Knockbrex, that possibly Rutherford is somewhat too full of ecstasy for this fallen, still unsanctified, and still so slippery world.

It took two men to carry back the cluster of grapes the spies cut down at Eshcol, and there is sweetness and strength and ecstasy enough for ten men in anyone of Rutherford's heaven-inebriated

Letters. 'See what the land is, and whether it be fat or lean, and bring back of the fruits of the land.' This was the order given by Moses to the twelve spies. And, whether the land was fat or lean, Moses and all Israel could judge for themselves when the spies laid down their load of grapes at Moses' feet. 'I can report nothing but good of the land,' said Joshua Redivivus, as he sent back such clusters of its vineyards and such pots of its honey to Hugh Mackail, to Marion McNaught, and to Lady Kenmure. And then, when all his letters were collected and published, never surely, since the Epistles of Paul and the Gospel and Revelation of John, had such clusters of encouragement and such exhilarating cordials been laid to the lips of the Church of Christ.

Our old authors tell us that after the northern tribes had tasted the warmth and the sweetness of the wines of Italy they could take no rest till they had conquered and taken possession of that land of sunshine where such grapes so plentifully grew. And how many hearts have been carried captive with the beauty and the grace of Christ, and with the land of Immanuel, where He drinks wine with the saints in His Father's house, by the reading of Samuel Rutherford's Letters, the day of the Lord will alone declare.

> O Christ! He is the Fountain,
> The deep sweet Well of love!
> The streams on earth I've tasted
> More deep I'll drink above.
> There to an ocean fullness
> His mercy doth expand,
> And glory, glory dwelleth
> In Immanuel's Land.

A story is told by Wodrow of an English merchant who had occasion to visit Scotland on business about the year 1650. On his return home his friends asked him what news he had brought with him from the north. 'Good news,' he said; 'for when I went to St. Andrews I heard a sweet, majestic-looking man, and he showed me the majesty of God. After him I heard a little fair man, and he showed me the loveliness of Christ. I then went to Irvine, where I heard a well-favoured, proper old man with a long beard, and that man showed me all my own heart.' What a feast of the Word he must have enjoyed! For the sweet, majestic-looking man was Robert Blair, of whom Dr. McCrie says that he had 'a mind deeply exercised about eternal things, and full of warm and manly piety.' The little fair man who showed this English merchant the loveliness of Christ was Samuel Rutherford, and the proper old man who showed him all his own heart was David Dickson who had seen a great awakening among his people in the early days of his ministry in the same parish of Irvine. Dr. McCrie says of David Dickson that he was singularly successful in dissecting the human heart and in winning souls to the Redeemer, and all that we know of Dickson bears out that high estimate. When he was presiding on one occasion at the ordination of a young minister, whom he had had some hand in bringing up, among the advices the old minister gave the new beginner were these: That he should remain unmarried for four years, in order to give himself up wholly to his great work; both in preaching and in prayer he should be as succinct as possible so as not to weary his hearers; and, lastly, 'Oh, study God well and your own heart.' We have five letters of Rutherford's to this master of the human heart, and it is in the third of these that Rutherford opens his heart to his father in the Gospel, and tells him that he is made up of extremes.

In every way that was so. It is a common remark with all Rutherford's biographers and editors and commentators what extremes met in that little fair man. The finest thing that has ever been written on Rutherford is Dr. Taylor Innes's lecture in the Evangelical Succession series. And the intellectual extremes that met in Rutherford are there set forth at some length by Rutherford's acute and sympathetic critic. For one thing, the greatest speculative freedom and theological breadth met in Rutherford with the greatest ecclesiastical hardness and narrowness. I do not know any author of that day, either in England or in Scotland, either Prelatist or Puritan, who shows more imaginative freedom and speculative power than Rutherford does in his *Christ Dying,* unless it is his still greater contemporary, Thomas Goodwin. And it is with corresponding distress that we read some of Rutherford's polemical works, and even the polemical parts of his heavenly Letters. There is a remarkable passage in one of his controversial books that reminds us of some of Shakespeare's own tributes to England: 'I judge that in England the Lord hath many names and a fair company that shall stand at the side of Christ when He shall render up the kingdom to the Father; and that in that renowned land there be men of all ranks, wise, valorous, generous, noble, heroic, faithful, religious, gracious, learned.' Rutherford's whole passage is worthy to stand beside Shakespeare's great passage on 'this blessed plot, this earth, this realm, this England.' But persecution from England and controversy at home so embittered Rutherford's sweet and gracious spirit that passages like that are but few and far between. Only, let him away out into pure theology, and, especially, let him get his wings on the person, and the work, and the glory of Christ, and few theologians of any age or any school rise to a larger air, or command a wider scope, or discover a clearer eye of speculation than Rutherford, till we feel exactly like the laird of Glanderston who, when Rutherford left a controversial passage in a sermon and went on to speak of Christ, cried out in the church: 'Ay, hold you there, minister; you are all right there!' A domestic controversy that arose in the Church of Scotland towards the end of Rutherford's life so separated Rutherford from Dickson and Blair that Rutherford would not take part with Blair, the 'sweet, majestic-looking man,' in the Lord's Supper. 'Oh, to be above,' Blair exclaimed, 'where there are no misunderstandings!' It was this same controversy that made John Livingstone say in a letter to Blair that his wife and he had had more bitterness over that dispute than ever they had tasted since they knew what bitterness meant. Well might Rutherford say, on another such occasion: 'It is hard when saints rejoice in the sufferings of saints, and when the redeemed hurt, and go nigh to hate the redeemed.' Watch and pray, my brethren, lest in controversy - ephemeral and immaterial controversy - you also go near to hate and hurt one another, as Rutherford did.

And then, what strength, combined with what tenderness, there is in Rutherford! In all my acquaintance with literature I do not know any author who has two books under his name so unlike one another, two books that are such a contrast to one another, as *Lex Rex* and the *Letters*. A more firmly built argument than *Lex Rex,* an argument so clamped together with the iron bands of scholastic and legal lore, is not to be met with in any English book; a more lawyer-looking production is not in all the Advocates' Library than just *Lex Rex*. There is as much emotion in the multiplication table as there is in *Lex Rex*; and then, on the other hand, the *Letters* have no other fault but this, that they are overcharged with emotion. The *Letters* would be absolutely perfect if they were only a little more restrained and chastened in this one respect. The pundit and the poet are the opposites and the extremes of one another; and the pundit and the poet meet, as nowhere else that I know of, in the author of *Lex Rex* and the *Letters*.

Then, again, what extremes of beauty and sweetness there are in Rutherford's style, too often intermingled with what carelessness and disorder. What flashes of noblest thought, clothed in the most apt and well-fitting words, on the same page with the most slatternly and down-at-the-heel English. Both Dr. Andrew Bonar and Dr. Andrew Thomson have given us selections from Rutherford's *Letters* that would quite justify us in claiming Rutherford as one of the best writers of English in his day; but then we know out of what thickets of careless composition these flowers have been collected. Both Gillespie and Rutherford ran a tilt at Hooker; but alas for the equipment and the manners of our champions when compared with the shining panoply and the knightly grace of the author of the incomparable *Polity.*

In one of the very last letters he ever wrote - his letter to James Guthrie in 1661 - he is still amazed that God has not brought his sin to the Market Cross, to use his own word. But all through his letters this same note of admiration and wonder runs - that he has been taken from among the pots and his wings covered with silver and gold. Truly, in his case the most seraphic saintliness was not forfeited, and we who read his books may well bless God it was so.

And then, experimentally also, what extremes met in our author! Pascal in Paris and Rutherford in Anwoth and Aberdeen and St. Andrews were at the very opposite poles ecclesiastically from one another. I do not like to think what Rutherford would have said of Pascal, but I cannot embody what I have to say of Rutherford's experimental extremes better than just by this passage taken from the *Thoughts*: 'The Christian religion teaches the righteous man that it lifts him even to a participation in the divine nature; but that, in this exalted state, he still bears within him the fountain of all corruption, which renders him during his whole life subject to error and misery, to sin and death, while at the same time it proclaims to the most wicked that they can still receive the grace of their Redeemer.' And again: 'Did we not know ourselves full of pride, ambition, lust, weakness, misery and injustice, we were indeed blind....What then can we feel but a great esteem for a religion that is so well acquainted with the defects of man, and a great desire for the truth of a religion that promises remedies so precious.'

And yet again, what others thought of him, and how they treated him, compared with what he knew himself to be, caused Rutherford many a bitter reflection. Every letter he got consulting him and appealing to him as if he had been God's living oracle made him lie down in the very dust with shame and self-abhorrence. Writing on one occasion to Robert Blair he told him that his letter consulting him about some matter of Christian experience had been like a blow in the face to him; "It affects me much," said Rutherford, "that a man like you should have any such opinion of me." And, apologising for his delay in replying to a letter of Lady Boyd's, he says that he is put out of all love of writing letters because his correspondents think things about him that he himself knows are not true. 'My white side comes out on paper - but at home there is much black work. All the challenges that come to me are true.' There was no man then alive on the earth so much looked up to and consulted in the deepest matters of the soul, in the secrets of the Lord with the soul, as Rutherford was, and his letters bear evidence on every page that there was no man who had a more loathsome and a more hateful experience of his own heart, not even Brodie, not even Owen, not even Bunyan, not even Baxter. What a day of extremest men that was, and what an inheritance we extreme men have had left us, in their inward, extreme, and heavenly books!

Once more, hear him on the tides of feeling that continually rose and fell within his heart. Writing from Aberdeen to Lady Boyd, he says: 'I have not now, of a long time, found such high springtides as formerly. The sea is out, and I cannot buy a wind and cause it to flow again; only I wait on the shore till the Lord sends a full sea.... But even to dream of Him is sweet.' And then, just over the leaf, to Marion McNaught: 'I am well: honour to God.... He hath broken in upon a poor prisoner's soul like the swelling of Jordan. I am bank and brim full: a great high springtide of the consolations of Christ hath overwhelmed me.' But sweet as it is to read his rapturous expressions when the tide is full, I feel it far more helpful to hear how he still looks and waits for the return of the tide when the tide is low, and when the shore is full, as all left shores are apt to be, of weeds and mire, and all corrupt and unclean things. Rutherford is never more helpful to his correspondents than when they consult him about their ebb tides, and find that he himself either has been, or still is, in the same experience.

But why do we disinter such things as these out of such an author as Samuel Rutherford? Why do we tell to all the world that such an eminent saint was full of such sad extremes? Well, we surely do so out of obedience to the divine command to comfort God's people; for, next to their having no such extremes in themselves, their next best comfort is to be told that great and eminent saints of God have had the very same besetting sins and staggering extremes as they still have. If the like of Samuel Rutherford was vexed and weakened with such intellectual contradictions and spiritual extremes in his mind, in his heart and in his history, then may we not hope that some such saintliness, if not some such service as his, may be permitted to us also?

Chapter Two

SELECTED SAYINGS OF SAMUEL RUTHERFORD

☙

Preachers and public speakers alike know that having a ready supply of quotations adds a strength and depth to the content of any sermon or speech.

W.E.Sangster advised, "It is when a preacher is offering an opinion upon a subject that is likely to create a controversy in the minds of his hearers, that a pertinent quotation in his own support is most useful. Even then it needs to be quoted under a great man."

This collection of quotations from the writings of Samuel Rutherford can be compared to a cup of refreshing water from a deep well, or like precious nuggets mined from a rich vein of gold.

Both his letters and his sermons are rich in proverbial sayings. They are filled with desires for Christ, comfort for the afflicted, and groaning after holiness. They provide wise counsel for both saint and sinner in every generation.

Affliction

❖ *When I am in the cellar of affliction, I look for the Lord's choicest wines.*

❖ *Sanctified afflictions lead men to God.*

❖ *There is no cross or misery that befalls the Church of God or any of His children, but God is related to it.*

❖ *The thorn is one of the most cursed and angry and crabbed weeds that the earth yields, and yet out of it springs the rose, one of the sweetest smelled flowers and most delightful to the eye.*

❖ *Well is them who are under crosses and Christ says to them, 'half-mine.'*

❖ *His loved ones are most tried; the lintel stones and pillars of His New Jerusalem suffer more knocks from God's hammer than the common side-wall stones.*

❖ *He delighteth to take up fallen bairns, and to mend broken brows.*

Assistance

❖ *It is vain for us to rise up early and to lie down late and to eat the bread of sorrow all the day, if the Lord gives not the assistance of His Spirit to the means that we use.*

❖ *If you seek, there is a hoard, a hidden treasure, and a gold mine in Christ you never yet saw.*

Assurance

❖ *Make much of assurance for it keepeth your anchor fixed.*

Bitterness

❖ *I find His sweet presence eateth out the bitterness of sorrow and suffering.*

Cheerfulness

❖ *I wonder many times that ever a child of God should have a sad heart, considering what the Lord is preparing for him.*

Christ

❖ *I know not a thing worth the buying but heaven; and my own mind is, if comparison were made betwixt Christ and heaven, I would sell heaven with my blessing, and buy Christ.*

❖ *Jesus Christ came into my prison cell last night and every stone flashed like a ruby.*

❖ *They lose nothing who gain Christ.*

❖ *Since He looked upon me my heart is not mine own, He hath run away to heaven with it!*

❖ *Christ is so good; I will have no other tutor, supposing I could have, and choice of ten thousand beside.*

❖ *My advice to you is, take a house next door to the Physician for it will be very singular if you should prove to be the very first He ever turned away unhealed.*

❖ *Ye heard of me the whole counsel of God. Sew no clouts upon Christ's robe. Take Christ in His rags and losses and as persecuted by men, and be content to sigh and pant up the mountains with Christ's cross upon your back.*

❖ *Christ is the sinner's Magna Carta.*

❖ *I would fain learn not to idolise comfort, serve joy and sweet felt pleasure ...the Bridegroom Himself is better than all the ornaments that are about Him.*

❖ *Once when Lord Kenmore asked 'What will Christ be like when He cometh?' Rutherford's reply was 'All lovely'.*

❖ *Oh if you saw the beauty of Jesus, and smelled the fragrance of His love, you would run through fire and water to be with Him.*

❖ *Christ is a well of life, but who knoweth how deep it is to the bottom?*

❖ *Living in the womb, the Ancient of days became young for me.*

❖ *Christ is man, but He is not like man.*

❖ *To live in Christ's love is a king's life.*

❖ *I know that you are looking to Christ and I beseech you to follow your look.*

Christians

❖ *He is like the man that has many kin and few friends. Many now are with Christ and few for Christ.*

Comfort

❖ *Courage! Up your heart! When ye do tire, He will bear both you and your burden. Yet a little while and ye shall see the salvation of God,*

❖ *Slip yourself under Christ's wing till the storm is over.*

Conscience

❖ *Hurt not your conscience with any known sin.*

❖ *We take nothing to the grave with us but a good or evil conscience.*

❖ *Keep the conscience whole without a crack.*

❖ *A good conscience is a good soft well-made bed.*

❖ *Alas, that so many are carried with the times! As if their conscience rolled upon oiled wheels, so do they go the way the wind bloweth them.*

Consecration

❖ *Oh how sweet to be wholly Christ's and wholly in Christ! To be out of the creatures owning and made complete in Christ!*

❖ *Happy is your soul if Christ mans the house, and takes the keys Himself, and commands all, as it suiteth Him full well to rule all wherever He is.*

Contentment

❖ *If contentment were here, heaven were not heaven.*

❖ *It is not safe to be at pulling and drawing with the omnipotent Lord. Let the pull go with Him, for He is strong; and say, 'Thy will be done.'*

Cross

❖ *The cross of Christ is the sweetest burden that ever I did bare; it is such a burden as wings are to a bird, or sails are to a ship, to carry me forward to my harbour.*

❖ *The cross of Christ on which He was extended, points, in the length of it, to Heaven and earth, reconciling them together; and in the breadth of it, to former and following ages, as being equally salvation to both.*

❖ *A cross for Christ should have another name; yea, a cross, especially when He cometh with His arms full of joys, is the happiest hard tree that was ever laid upon my weak shoulder.*

❖ *Take His cross with Him cheerfully. Christ and His cross are not separable in this life; howbeit, Christ and His cross part at Heaven's door, for there is no houseroom for crosses in heaven.*

❖ *You will not get leave to steal quietly to heaven in Christ's company, without a conflict and a cross.*

❖ *Crosses are proclaimed as common accidents to all the saints, and in them standeth a part of our communion with Christ.*

❖ *Neither need we fear crosses, or sigh or be sad for anything that is on this side of heaven, if we have Christ.*

❖ *Our crosses would not bite us if we were heavenly minded.*

❖ *When Christ blesseth His own crosses with a tongue, they breathe out Christ's love, wisdom, kindness, and care for us.*

❖ *The weightiest end of the cross of Christ that is laid upon you lieth upon your strong Saviour.*

❖ *Put your hand to the pen, and let the cross of your Lord Jesus have your submissive and resolute Amen.*

❖ *I would wish each cross were looked in the face seven times and were read over and over again. It is the messenger of the Lord and speaks something.*

❖ *Christ and His cross together are sweet company and a blessed couple.*

❖ *Christ hath borne the whole complete cross and His saints bear but bits and chips; as the apostle saith, 'the remnants or leavings of the cross.'*

❖ *No man hath a velvet cross.*

Death

❖ *The distance between us and Christ is death.*

❖ *Death is Christ's ferryboat to carry the Christian home.*

❖ *Christ's gain is not your loss.*

❖ *O happy and blessed death, that golden bridge laid over by Christ my Lord, between time's clay banks and heaven's shore.*

❖ *How you will rejoice when Christ drieth your face, and welcometh you to glory and happiness.*

Dedication

❖ *You will not be carried to Heaven lying at ease upon a feather bed.*

❖ *Because I am His own (God be thanked) He may use me as He pleaseth.*

❖ *Let Him make anything out of me, so being He be glorified in my salvation: for I know I am made for Him.*

Division

❖ *It is a fearful sin to make a rent and a hole in Christ's mystical body because there is a spot in it.*

❖ *Woe is unto us for these sad divisions that make us lose the fair scent of the Rose of Sharon.*

Election

❖ *If so be that freewill were our tutor, and we had our heaven in our own keeping, then we would lose all. But because we have Christ for our tutor and He has our heaven in His hand, therefore the covenant must be perpetual.*

Fainting

❖ *Faint not; the miles to heaven are few and short. There are many heads lying in Christ's bosom, but there is room for yours among the rest.*

Faith

❖ *True faith is humble, and seeth no way to escape but only in Christ.*

❖ *My faith hath no bed to rest upon but omnipotency.*

❖ *A little faith lays hold on an eternal redemption and everlasting righteousness, as well as strong faith.*

❖ *A little hand with small fingers may receive a great Heaven and lay hold on the great Saviour of the world.*

❖ *The spirit sets faith a-going and makes it move sweetly on wheels oiled with the love of Christ and His apprehended beauty and fairness.*

❖ *Faith fetches its food from afar; it gathers life, growth and strength by exercising itself in frequent visions and acts of beholding Christ.*

❖ *I believe faith will teach you to kiss a striking Lord.*

❖ *Faith apprehendeth pardon, but never payeth a penny for it.*

❖ *How soon would faith freeze without a cross?*

❖ *It is faith's work to claim and challenge loving kindness out of all the roughest strokes of God.*

❖ *Faith is exceeding charitable and believeth no evil in God.*

❖ *Faith's eyes can see through a millstone.*

❖ *The scarcity of faith in the earth said, "We are hard upon the last nick of time:" Blessed are those who keep their garments clean, against the Bridegroom's coming.*

❖ *Consent and say "Amen" to the promises, and ye have sealed that God is true and Christ is yours. This is an easy market. Ye but look on with faith; for Christ suffered all, and paid all.*

Glory

❖ *Christ was greedy of glory to Him that sent Him.*

Gospel

❖ *The Gospel is like a small hair that hath breadth, and will not cleave in two*

Grace

❖ *Grace withereth without adversity.*

❖ *Grace grows best in winter.*

❖ *Grace was in Him as a river. He could not keep it within the banks; it must flow over to needy sinners.*

❖ *Grace tried is better than grace, and it is more than grace; it is glory in its infancy.*

❖ *I know no sweeter way to heaven than through free grace and hard trials together; and one of these cannot well want another.*

Heaven

❖ *We are as near heaven as we are far from self, and far from the love of a sinful world.*

❖ *If His love was not in heaven, I should be unwilling to go thither.*

❖ *God hath made many flowers, but the fairest of them all is heaven, and the flower of all flowers is Christ.*

❖ *Go up beforehand and see your lodging. Look through all your Father's rooms in heaven; in your Father's house are many dwelling places. Men take a sight of lands ere they buy them. I know Christ hath made the bargain already: but be kind to the house you are going to, and see it often.*

Hope

❖ *Better God's heirs live upon hope than upon hire.*

❖ *The hope of heaven under troubles is like wind and sails to the soul.*

Humility

❖ *Humility is a strange flower; it grows best in winter weather and under storms of affliction.*

❖ *There cannot be a more humble soul than a believer. It is no pride in a drowning man to catch hold of a rock nor for a ship-broken soul to run himself ashore upon Christ.*

❖ *Stoop! It is a low entry to go in at heaven's gate.*

Jews

❖ *O to see the sight, next to Christ's second coming in the clouds, the most joyful! Our elder brethren the Jews and Christ fall upon one another's necks and kiss each other.*

Loneliness

❖ *Ye are now alone, but ye may have for the seeking, three always in your company, the Father, Son and Holy Spirit: I trust they are near you.*

Lordship

❖ *Let Christ have a commanding power and a King-throne in you.*

Love

❖ *Get love and no burden Christ will lay on you will be heavy.*

❖ *I love Christ to worst reproaches.*

❖ *Everyday we may see some new thing in Christ; His love hath neither brim nor bottom.*

❖ *Look upon Him and love Him. Oh love and live.*

❖ *Christ's love is young glory and young heaven.*

❖ *Love is a beam from the eternal Son of Righteousness.*

❖ *Love would have the company of the party loved; and my greatest pain is the want of Him, not of His joys and comforts, but of a near union and communion.*

❖ *Keep yourself in the love of Christ, and stand far back from the pollutions of the world.*

❖ *Put Christ's love to the trial, and put upon it our burdens, and then it will appear love indeed. We employ not His love, and therefore we know it not.*

Obedience

❖ *That piece of service, believing in a smiting Redeemer, is a precious part of obedience.*

Old Age

❖ *Old age and waxing old as a garment is written on the fairest of creation.*

Patience

❖ *Give the Lord time to work; His end is underground.*

Perseverance

❖ *Venture to take the wind on your face for Christ.*

Praise

❖ *I would praise Him for this, that the whole army of the redeemed ones sit rent-free in Heaven.*

Prayer

❖ *Prayer without faith is but pagan service and the voice of dogs howling for hunger.*

❖ *I have been benefited by praying for others; for by making myself an errand to God for them I have gotten something for myself.*

❖ *Set no time to the Lord the Creator of life, for His time is always best.*

❖ *Praying is a grace and must be fathered and bottomed on grace.*

❖ *I shall rather spill twenty prayers than not pray at all. Let my broken words go up to heaven; when they come into the great Angel's golden censer, that compassionate Advocate will put together my broken prayers and perfume them.*

❖ *Prayer is like God's file to stir a rusty heart.*

❖ *Lighten your heart by laying your all upon Him.*

❖ *Words are but the body, the garment, the outside of prayer; sighs are nearer the heart work. A dumb beggar getteth an alms at Christ's gates, even by making signs, when his tongue cannot plead for him; and the rather, because he is dumb...Tears have a tongue, and grammar, and language, that our Father knoweth. Babes have no prayer for the breast, but weeping: the mother can read hunger in weeping.*

❖ *Send the heavy heart up to Christ, it shall be welcome.*

❖ *It is our heaven to lay many weights and burdens upon Christ.*

Preaching

❖ *Next to Christ I had but one joy – to preach Christ my Lord.*

Pride

❖ *Our pride must have winter weather to rot it.*

Prosperity

❖ *Build your nest upon no tree here; for you see God hath sold the forest to death.*

Providence

❖ *Let God make of you what He will.   He will end all with consolation and will make glory out of your suffering.*

❖ *Providence hath a thousand keys to open a thousand sundry doors for the deliverance of His own, when it is even come to a desperate case. Let us be faithful; and care for our own part, which is to do and suffer for Him, and lay Christ's part on Himself, and leave it there.*

Refuge

❖ *I creep under my Lord's wings in the great shower, and the water cannot reach me.*

Repentance

❖ *A repenting man is more angry at his own heart that consenteth to sin, than he is at the devil who did tempt him to sin.*

❖ *Repentance is a work of grace, and not misery.*

❖ *If ye never had a sick night and a pained soul for sin, ye have not yet lighted upon Christ.*

Reproach

❖ *I love Christ's reproaches.*

Rest

❖ *There is a rest for the people of God. Christ possesseth it now one thousand six hundred years before many of His members; but it weareth not out.*

Reward

❖ *Howbeit this day be not yours and Christ's, the morrow will be yours and His. I would not exchange the joy of my bonds and imprisonment for Christ, with all the joy of this dirty and foul-skinned world.*

Saints

❖ *The saints are little pieces of mystical Christ.*

❖ *The saints, at their best, are but strangers to the weight and worth of the incomparable sweetness of Christ.*

Salvation

❖ *That Christ and a forgiven sinner should be made one and share heaven between them, is the wonder of salvation; what more could love do?*

❖ *Who could be saved if God were not God, and if He were not such a God as He is?*

❖ *I disclaim all. The port I would be in is redemption and forgiveness of sin through His blood.*

❖ *Our salvation is fastened with God's own hand, and with Christ's own strength, to the strong stake of God's unchangeable nature.*

❖ *When I look to my guiltiness, I see that my salvation is one of my Saviour's greatest miracles, either in Heaven or earth; I am sure I may defy any man to show me a greater wonder.*

❖ *I am Christ's sworn bankruptcy, to whom He will entrust nothing; no, not one pin in the work of my salvation. Let me stand in black and white in the bankrupt roll before Christ. I am happy that my salvation is accredited to Christ's mediation.*

Sanctification

❖ *Take Christ for sanctification, as well as justification.*

❖ *Christ is but seeking a clean glistening bride out of the fire.*

❖ *If you would be a deep divine, I recommend to you sanctification.*

❖ *Sanctification and the mortification of our lusts are the hardest part of Christianity.*

Satan

❖ *The devil's war is better than the devil's peace. Suspect dumb holiness; when the dog is kept out of doors he howls to be let in again.*

❖ *Satan is only God's master fencer to teach us to use our weapons.*

❖ *The devil is like the barking dog that scatters the sheep. Separation from the assembly of the saints is not of God.*

Self

❖ *Oh, wretched idol, myself.*

❖ *He looketh to what I desire to be, and not to what I am.*

Sickness

❖ *It is a blessed fever that fetcheth Christ to the bedside.*

Sifting

❖ *God's wheat in this land must go through Satan's sieve.*

Sin

❖ *Sin's joys are but night dreams, thoughts, imaginations and shadows.*

❖ *Woe to the sinner that gets that which falls to him, and is his due, for that is hell!*

❖ *Be sorry at your corruption.*

❖ *Sin poisons all our enjoyments.*

❖ *Put off a sin, or a piece of sin, every day.*

❖ *Labour constantly for a sound and lively sense of sin.*

Sorrow

❖ *Ye have lost a child, she is not lost to you who is found in Christ; she is not sent away, but only sent before, like a star which, going out of sight, does not die and vanish, but shines in another hemisphere.*

❖ *It is not for nothing that ye have lost one on earth. There hath been too little of your love and heart in heaven, and therefore the jealousy of Christ hath done this.*

❖ *If the place she hath left were any other than a prison of sin, and the home she is gone to any other than where her Head and Saviour is King of the land, your grief had been more rational.*

Soul winning

❖ *Take as many to heaven with you as ye are able to draw. The more ye draw with you; ye will be the welcomer yourself. Be no niggard, or sparing churl, of the grace of God.*

Spiritual Dryness

❖ *Dry wells send us to the fountain.*

❖ *We dwell far from the well, and complain but dryly of our dryness and dullness: we are rather dry than thirsty.*

Spiritual Growth

❖ *I am like a child that hath a golden book, and playeth more with the ribbons and the gilding and the picture in the first page, than reading the contents of it.*

Suffering

❖ *Suffering is the other half of our ministry, howbeit the hardest.*

❖ *To suffer for Christ is the garland and flower of all crosses.*

❖ *Scar not at suffering for Christ, for Christ hath a chair and a cushion and sweet peace for a sufferer.*

❖ *Sanctified straits cause the conies to run into their rocks for refuge, as many lost strangers from God learn the gate to Christ by their sufferings.*

❖ *It is folly to think to steal to heaven with a whole skin.*

Temptation

❖ *To want temptation is the greatest temptation of all.*

❖ *Temptations that I supposed to have been struck dead and laid upon their back rise again and revive upon me; yea, I see that while I live temptations will not die.*

❖ *Flee the follies of youth: ply the merchant for ye cannot expect another market day when this is done.*

Trials

❖ *They lose nothing who gain Christ.*

❖ *Saints must be best in worst times.*

❖ *I bless the Lord that all our troubles come through Christ's fingers, and that He casteth sugar among them, and casteth in some ounce weights of Heaven, and of the spirit of glory that resteth on suffering believers, into one cup, in which there is no taste of hell.*

❖ *Take ease to thyself, and let Him bear all.*

❖ *Why should I tremble at the plough of my Lord that maketh deep furrows on my soul? I know He is no idle husbandman; He purposeth a crop.*

❖ *We live in a sea where many have suffered shipwreck, and have need that Christ sits at the helm of the ship.*

❖ *My chains are over gilded with gold.*

❖ *Oh what I owe to the file, to the hammer, to the furnace of my Lord Jesus!*

Truth

❖ *Serve Christ; back Him; let His cause be your cause; give not a hairsbreadth of truth away, for it is not yours but God's.*

❖ *It is common for men to make doubts when they have the mind to desert the truth.*

❖ *When the truth is come to your hand, hold it fast; go not again to make a new search and inquiry for truth. It is easy to cause conscience to believe as ye will, not as ye know.*

Unbelief

❖ Unbelief is always an irrational thing.

Victory

❖ *The thing that we mistake is the want of victory; we hold that to be the mark of one who hath no grace. Nay, I say, the want of fighting were a mark of no grace; but I shall not say the want of victory is such a mark.*

Wants

❖ *Wants are my best riches, because I have these supplied by Christ.*

Warfare

❖ *I look not to win away to my home without wounds and blood.*

❖ *They are not worthy of Jesus who will not take a blow for their Master's sake.*

Watchfulness

❖ *There is as much need to watch over grace as to watch over sin.*

Well-done

❖ *His 'well done' is worth a shipful of 'good-days' and earthly honours.*

Witness

❖ *Make others to see Christ in you; moving, doing, speaking and thinking.*

World

❖ *When the race is ended and the play is either won or lost, and you are in the utmost circle and border of time, and shall put your foot within the march of eternity, all the good things of your short night dreams shall seem to you like ashes of a blaze of thorns or straw.*

❖ *This world never looked like a friend upon you. Ye owe it little love. It looked ever sour like upon you. Howbeit you should woo it, it will not match with you; and therefore never seek warm fire under cold ice. This is not a field where your happiness groweth; it is up above.*

❖ *If we were not strangers here, the dogs of the world would not bark at us.*

❖ *As a child cannot hold two apples in his little hand, but the one putteth the other out of its room, so neither can we be master of two loves.*

❖ *This world is a great forest of thorns on your way to heaven, but you must go through it.*

❖ *Let all the world be nothing and let God be all things.*

❖ *The world deserveth nothing but the outer court of our soul.*

Chapter Three

LIVING INSIGHTS & ILLUSTRATIONS

☉

This collection of living insights and illustrations is gleaned from a wide variety of sources. It introduces some highlights of Samuel Rutherford's life from the time when, as a young child of three years of age he had a near encounter with death when he fell down the village well and was rescued by 'a bonnie white man'; until early in the spring of 1661 when he was summoned by the 'Drunken Parliament' to appear before the bar of the house to answer charges of treason. His reply to the messenger who brought the summons as he lay on his deathbed was,

> "I have got a summons to appear before a superior Judge and Judiciary, and it behoves me to answer my first summons, and ere your day arrive I shall be where few kings and great folks come."

His remarkable life was as colourful as his preaching. These carefully chosen anecdotes provide a rich storehouse of material for the busy preacher, and will enable you to become better acquainted with the story of Rutherford's life and help you to appreciate why he was described as 'The Saint of the Covenant.'

In 1627 Rutherford was licensed as a preacher of the gospel and soon received a call to the little church of Anwoth in the Stewartry of Kirkcudbright. Anwoth was not altogether virgin soil for the seed of the gospel, for John Welsh had been at Kirkcudbright from 1595 until 1600, when he then moved to Ayr. Welsh was son-in-law of John Knox and a man of truly apostolic zeal and labour. He and Robert Bruce of Kinnaird were the most powerful ministers of the time in Scotland. He was 'famous in his generation' as one who was mighty in prayer and whose *cri de coeur* found voice in the words: 'O God, wilt Thou not give me Scotland! O God, wilt Thou not give me Scotland!' He kept a warm plaid by his bed to wrap round his body when he rose in the night to pray and there were times when his wife would entreat him to desist. But his answer was aye the same: he had that to press him which she had not; he had the souls of three thousand to answer for, and he knew not how it was with many of them. In 1605, he was imprisoned in Blackness Castle and in 1606 he was driven into exile to France. Late in 1621, he was informed that if he chose he might return to London 'to be dealt with'. He came, and his wife was admitted to an audience with James I. The King asked her who her father had been, and she replied, 'John Knox'.

'Knox and Welsh!' he exclaimed; 'the devil never made sic a match as that!'

'It's right like Sir,' said she, 'for we never speared (asked) his advice.'

He then asked how many of John Knox's children were still alive, and if they were lads or lasses. She told him that there were three, and that they were all lasses.

'God be thanked,' cried the king, lifting up both his hands, 'for if they had been three lads, I had never buiked (enjoyed) my three kingdoms in peace.'

She urged the king to let her husband return to Scotland and to give him his native air.

'Give him his native air!' said James; 'give him the devil!'

But her wit flashed out with indignation as she rejoined: 'Give that to your hungry courtiers!'

The King at last said that he could return if he would first submit to the bishops. She lifted her apron, held it out, and made reply in her father's spirit. 'Please Your Majesty, I'd rather kep his head there.'

John Welsh died in London in April 1622, and it was long remembered how he had cried on his deathbed in an ecstasy of sweet communion: 'Hold, Lord! Enough; I can bear no more.'

Of Rutherford's early youth we know little beyond the story told by Robert Wodrow, of a narrow escape from drowning which he had in his infancy. As a child of four, he had been playing with an elder sister near their home when he fell into a deep well. Unable to rescue him herself, his sister ran to their father and mother for help. When the alarmed parents reached the well however, they found young Samuel sitting on the grass beside it little the worse for his sudden immersion. He had been rescued, he declared, by a "bonnie white man," who had pulled him out of the well by the hand. This story has often been told as suggesting an early awareness on Rutherford's part of a spiritual world, but it is unwise to insist that it has any such significance. The deliverer was in all probability a modest hero of the countryside, perhaps neither "bonnie" nor "white", save in the eyes of the rescued child. But he performed a service in which even an angel might well have taken a holy pride when he delivered the coming Covenanter from an early death.

Rutherford's ministry while in Anwoth was a noble approach to the splendid ideal of Baxter's 'Reformed Pastor' or Herbert's 'Country Parson'. His first sermon had been based on the text: 'And Jesus said, For judgement I am come into this world, that they which

see not might see; and that they which see might be made blind'
(John 9 v.39). His great desire as a preacher was that he might help
those who saw not, to see the King and to dwell in His city. Yet it
was long before he could convince himself that there was tangible
evidence of true and definite conversions. We still hear his wistful
lament two years after he had begun his work in the parish: 'I see
exceeding small fruit of my ministry, and would be glad to know of
one soul to be my crown and rejoicing in the day of Christ.' That
thirst for souls never left him; it consumed his spirit even when in
exile. 'My witness is above,' he cried; 'your heaven would be two
heavens to me, and the salvation of you all as two salvations to me.'
Was it so strange that his name should have spread beyond the borders
of Anwoth until it rang up and down in all the farms and valleys of
the Lowlands?

At one time Archbishop Usher visited Scotland, and hearing much
of the piety of the Rev. Samuel Rutherford, resolved on being a
witness of it. Disguised as a pauper, on a Saturday evening he
solicited lodging for the night. Mr. Rutherford took him in, and
directed him to be seated in the kitchen. Mrs. Rutherford catechised
the servants, as a preparation for the Sabbath; and having asked the
stranger the number of the Divine commandments, he answered
eleven. The good woman hastily concluded him ignorant, and said,
"What a shame it is for you, a man with grey hairs, in a Christian
country, not to know how many commandments there are! There is
not a child six years old in this parish, but could answer the question
properly." Lamenting his condition, she ordered his supper, and
directed a servant to show him a bed in the garret. Mr. Rutherford
having heard him at prayer, and finding out whom he was, prevailed
on the Archbishop to preach for him, which he agreed to do, on
condition that he should not be made known. Early in the morning,
Mr. Rutherford changed his clothes, suffered him to depart, and
afterwards introduced him to breakfast as a minister on a journey.
When in the pulpit, he announced his text – "A new commandment
I give unto you, that ye love one another;" and remarked that this

might be reckoned the eleventh commandment. Mrs. Rutherford, remembering the answer she had received the night before from the stranger, was astonished, and looking at the preacher, almost imagined he might be the pitied traveller. The two holy men spent the evening in delightful conversation, and the Archbishop departed undiscovered, early on the following day.

The walls of the Old Church of Anwoth, though roofless and in ruins still remain. This is Samuel Rutherford's church, built for him in 1626, and therefore a shrine of undying interest. There is no sweeter or sadder spot in Scotland. The martyr, John Bell of Whitesyde, who was shot along with four others, was buried in the churchyard, and a flat tombstone records that he was shot at the command of Grier of Lagg, in 1685.

A new church has been built since; but the heritors, much to their honour, have preserved the ancient venerated building. It is of a barn like appearance, the length being of 64 feet, 7 inches; the width, 18 feet, 3 inches; the side walls only 10 feet; and calculated to hold not above 250 sitters, exclusive of small galleries, which are of comparatively recent erection. The pulpit is of oak, and is the very one out of which the celebrated subject of these pages preached. His stipend consisted of 200 merks Scots, about £11 sterling, derived from the tenants of the parish, and of a voluntary contribution on the part of his hearers.

Robert Blair relates in his autobiography that on returning from London to Ireland, via Portpatrick, he had a desire to visit Rutherford at Anwoth and Marion McNaught at Kirkcudbright. Not knowing how to compass both, when he came to the parting of the way he laid the bridle upon the horse's neck, "entreating the Lord to direct the horse as He saw meet." The horse took the way to Kirkcudbright, "where I found them both whom I desired to see, and was greatly refreshed with their company."

The story is told that Rutherford, on finding some young lads desecrating the Sabbath by playing football near the church, rebuked them, and set up three big stones as a testimony against such conduct. These stones were long known as "Rutherford's Witnesses". It is also said that some workmen who were building a new dyke on the farm of Mossrobin, were in want of stones for their work and one of them, who was a profane character, proposed making use of the said stones. His fellow workmates rejected the proposition with horror, and the man, stimulated by the bad ambition of showing himself superior to the fear of God wished, with dreadful imprecations, that the first morsel he took might choke him, if he did not build one of the stones into the dyke before breakfast. He accordingly broke up the stone, and accomplished his threat; but the story adds that on sitting down to his meal, and putting the first morsel into his mouth, he suddenly turned black in the face, fell back and expired. Needless to say the two other 'Witnesses' remain until this day. Such is the story, and it points to the more than superhuman power with which his parishioners credited their minister.

Another anecdote relating to those years in Anwoth, concerns his patron, John Gordon of Lochinvar. Gordon sprang from an old Galloway family and was born in 1599. His youth had been wild and lawless, but while abroad in France he had been brought to a better mind by John Welsh. On his return, he was friendly to the Presbyterian cause, but was absorbed in his lands and riches. 'Sometimes' John Howie says, 'he would be filled with a sense of sin which he was scarcely able to hold out against.' It was about 1626 that he married Lady Jane Campbell, the third daughter of the Earl of Argyll, and they lived at Rusco in the parish of Anwoth during the first two years of Rutherford's ministry. It was a great disappointment for him when they left for England late in September 1629. 'I have received many and divers dashes and heavy strokes since the Lord called me to the ministry,' he wrote, 'but indeed I esteem your departure from us amongst the weightiest.'

At the end of 1631 they were back in Scotland at Kenmure Castle some twenty miles from Anwoth. Rutherford was well aware of the weak point in Gordon's character and in April 1633, he warned his wife, 'Madam, stir up your husband to lay hold upon the Covenant and to do good. What hath he to do with the world? It is not his inheritance.' The test soon came, for he was made Viscount Kenmure and Lord Gordon of Lochinvar on the visit of Charles I to Edinburgh in June of that year. But he withdrew from the city on the pretext of an illness in order to avoid conflict between the king's favour and a tender conscience. A year later he was struck down with real illness, and was filled with remorse. Rutherford had been away from home, and he broke his journey on the way back to call at the Castle. Kenmure saw the finger of God in this, and in fear of death 'drew on a conference with the minister.' Peace of mind came for a while, but it was superficial. 'Dig deeper,' urged the faithful pastor, until at last he got down to the Rock. He was dying, but his farewell words of counsel to friends were not only treasured but were published long afterwards by Rutherford in *The Last Heavenly Speeches and Glorious Departure of John, Viscount Kenmure.* As the sun was setting on 12 September 1634 Rutherford engaged once more in prayer at his request; and as the words of prayer faded into silence, Lord Kenmure passed gently away.

It happened that James Guthrie – who was Minister successively at Lauder and Stirling ere he died a martyr's death at the Mercat Cross of Edinburgh in 1661 – had as his guest a man who, more than most of his contemporaries, was to leave his mark for good upon Scotland's national Church.

James Guthrie's guest was pre-eminently a man of prayer whose life was strictly regulated in accordance with Divine precept, yet, on the occasion to which we refer, he failed to act in full conformity with the golden rule of private prayer. He entered his closet, neglecting to shut the door with the result that he was overheard. A maid servant in the Manse, passing his door, saw him walking up and down the room so engrossed in meditation that he was quite unaware of her presence. It may be suspected that the maid lingered by the open door longer than the proprieties would have allowed, for she heard three petitions from the suppliant, which were spoken at quite considerable intervals. "Lord," he exclaimed, "make me believe in Thee!" He sat down and mused awhile and then, resuming his perambulations, spoke again. "Lord, make me love Thee!" There was another pause and then another petition, "Lord, make me keep all Thy commandments!"

Were these petitions granted? For answer, it is only necessary to mention that the petitioner was Samuel Rutherford!

It was said by Patrick Simpson, one of Rutherford's contemporaries, "He had two quick eyes, and when he walked it was observed that he held aye his face upward and heavenward. He had a strange utterance in the pulpit; a kind of shriek or scream that I never heard the like of. Many times I thought he would have flown out of the pulpit when he came to speak of Jesus Christ, and he never was in his right element but when he was commending him."

His hallowed life left memories in men's minds for many years. An enthusiast was found resting all night on his grave in the hope of inspiration; another would never pass the house in which Rutherford was born without raising his hat; and a workman preferred dismissal to obeying his master and removing some of the stones of the house in which Rutherford lived, when it was being dismantled.

During his banishment to Aberdeen the silence which was imposed upon him was his heaviest cross, and some of the allusions in his letters to his pulpit and parish work are exceedingly pathetic, e.g.: "I am for the present thinking the sparrows and swallows that build their nests at Anwoth blessed birds;" and again, "Oh, if I might but speak to three of four herd-boys of my worthy Master, I would be satisfied to be the meanest and most obscure of all the pastors in this land, and to live in any place, in any of Christ's basest outhouses." Such was his earnestness for the good of his people that he declares "his soul was taken up, when others were sleeping, how to have Christ betrothed with a bride in that part of the land;" and that "he wrestled with the angel and prevailed, and woods and trees and meadows and hills were his witnesses that he drew on a fair match (marriage) betwixt Christ and Anwoth."

When Rutherford resigned as Regent of Humanity at the University of Edinburgh he was already thinking of the ministry, and in preparation for it he devoted two years to the study of theology at the University. Very soon after being licensed as a preacher he received a call to Anwoth, where there had been no settled ministry for some years as a new church was due to be built; John Livingstone had already been called there but owing to the delay in building he had gone to Torpichen. "But thereafter," said Livingstone himself, "the Lord provided a great deal better for them, for they got that worthy servant of Christ, Mr. Samuel Rutherford, whose praise is in all the Reformed Churches."

Rutherford was a staunch Covenanter but controversy, though he excelled in it, seemed to be alien to his nature. One day, when preaching in Edinburgh, after dwelling for some time on the differences of the day, he broke out with – 'Woe is unto us for these sad divisions, that make us lose the fair scent of the Rose of Sharon!' And then he went on commending Christ, going over all his precious styles and titles for about a quarter of an hour; upon which the laird of Glanderston said, in a loud whisper, 'Ay, now you are right – hold you there!' However much Rutherford would like to have done so, in the prevailing conditions it was impossible. As a theologian and an ecclesiastic he worked out from his own centre - Christ. This is what entitles him to the epithet – 'a full-orbed saint'.

Horatius Bonar wrote of Rutherford: "There are not a few, who are so occupied with truth that they forget 'the true one'. When we consider how much of Rutherford's days were spent in contending for the truth; how much of his time was taken up with scholastic debate; how much of his attention was given to public affairs it is all the more wonderful to note that none of these things were allowed to interfere with his personal relationship to Christ. The more we become acquainted with the whole story of Rutherford's life the more fitted we are to come to a true estimate of the greatness of *the saint of the Covenant."*

In 1638, the General Assembly decided to appoint Rutherford to the Chair of Divinity in St. Mary's College in St. Andrews. During his time there his influence over the young men who attended his classes was great in providing a godly and pious generation of ministers who would strengthen the people of Scotland for the days of persecution that lay ahead. One of his first converts at this time was William Guthrie, who was well known for his book *The Christian's Great Interest,* and of whom John Owen declared: "That author I take to have been one of the greatest divines that ever wrote. It is my *vade-mecum."*

Rutherford's *Lex Rex* cut at the root of Stuart absolutism. He declared that absolute power was a fit garland only for the Infinite Majesty. It is one of the ablest pleas in defence of a constitutional form of government ever written. "The ordered liberties of the English speaking world are to this day the outcome of that teaching in regard to civil rights and obedience to which the Reformed tradition in Scotland led the writer of *Lex Rex.*" It is customary to talk of philosophy, but, as Hector Macpherson points out, the essence of his teaching is found in Rutherford's book written fifty years before. How strange to have the political textbook of the Covenant written by "the Saint of the Covenant!" Or is it, when we consider the issues at stake.

A young man of great ability, a Mr. Alexander Jameson, competed with an acquaintance of Rutherford's for the post of Regent in the College. They were equal in their trials, and 'the matter came to the determination of a lot.' The Principal, 'who was a little suspected of his piety and principles,' engaged in prayer, the lot was cast, and the appointment fell to Jameson. "Mr. Rutherford was extremely stormy at this, and says, 'Sirs, the prayer was not right gone about, and therefore the determination is not to be sisted on.' And without any more he rises up and prays himself, and the lot was casten over again, and it fell upon Mr. Jameson again. This perfectly confounded Mr. Rutherford, and no doubt let him see his rashness and error, and immediately he turned to Mr. Jameson and said, 'Sir, put on your gown, you have a better right to it than I have to mine.' And after that Rutherford and Jameson on nearer acquaintance were extraordinarily intimate and big."

In a debate on Church autonomy, the learned John Selden had delivered a masterly speech in favour of the Erastian view that ultimate authority for ecclesiastical matters was vested in the civil power. His arguments seemed decisive. But George Gillespie, Rutherford's close friend and companion, had been busy with his pen while Selden was on his feet, and as soon as Selden sat down, Rutherford whispered; "Rise George, rise and defend the right of the Lord Jesus Christ to govern the Church which he has purchased with His own blood." Gillespie responded with a speech that utterly demolished the arguments of his great antagonist. When he sat down, Selden remarked: "That young man by his single speech has swept away the learning and labour of ten years of my life." His friends seized the scrap of paper on which he was supposed to have written his notes; but the only thing they could find was the prayer which he had written again and again: 'Da lucem, Domine!' 'Give light, O Lord!'

Rutherford shone in humility, and always thought meanly of himself and highly of other ministers. Though he was Principal of the New College and chief Professor, yet he would always endeavour to set before him, worthy Mr. Robert Blair who was then minister of the town of St. Andrews. If he had been sitting in the church or any other place, he would have risen to have given him the place, and Mr. Blair would have frowned on him to sit down and keep his own place, and that because Mr. Blair was the elder minister. He had such a high esteem of worthy Mr. Blair that he never used to call him 'Brother' but only 'Sir' when he spoke to him.

A domestic controversy that arose in the Church of Scotland towards the end of Rutherford's life so separated Rutherford from Dickson and Blair that Rutherford would not take part with Blair, the 'sweet majestic-looking man,' in the Lord's Supper. 'Oh, to be above,' Blair exclaimed, 'where there are no misunderstandings!' It was this same controversy that made John Livingstone say in a letter to Blair that his wife and he had had more bitterness over that dispute than ever they had tasted since they knew what bitterness meant. Well might Rutherford say, on another such occasion: 'It is hard when saints rejoice in the sufferings of saints, and when the redeemed hurt, and go nigh to hate the redeemed.'

Once Rutherford had crowned Christ as Saviour and King of his own life his desire was that Scotland might do the same. "O blessed hands that shall put the crown upon Christ's head in Scotland." All the controversies in which he was engaged during the remainder of his life were in some way connected with the crown rights of the Redeemer. Whether against Armenians or Erastians, Stuart despots or Independents, it was always for "Zion's King and Zion's cause" that he did contend. "Serve Christ; back Him; let His cause be your cause; give not an hairbreadth of truth away, for it is not yours but God's." These words of exhortation to one of his correspondents are typical of Rutherford's own life. Having once established what Christ's cause and truth really were he refused to surrender one inch of territory to the enemy or give one hairbreadth of truth away. To do so would be disloyal to his Master. And with Rutherford that was unthinkable.

On the afternoon of the 28th March 1661 Rutherford said: "This night shall close the door and put my anchor within the vail, and I shall go away in a sleep by five o'clock in the morning." Over the Firth at Edinburgh the Drunken Parliament were busy that afternoon passing the Act Rescissory, that was to plunge the Kirk of Scotland into the blood and tears of a bitter persecution. But God "hid Samuel Rutherford with Himself from the wrangling and cruelty of wicked men." With the dawn of the 29th March, "it was said unto him, 'Come up hither': and the renowned eagle took his flight unto the Mountain of Spices."

Rutherford's body was buried within the grounds of the old Cathedral at St. Andrews. The following lines were inscribed on his tombstone:

> What tongue or pen or skill of men
> Can Famous Rutherford commend?
> His learning justly raised his Fame,
> True godliness adorned his name.
> He did converse with things above,
> Acquainted with Immanuel's love.
> Most orthodox he was and sound
> And many errors did confound.
> For Zion's King and Zion's cause
> And Scotland's covenanted laws
> Most constantly he did contend
> Until his time was at an end.
> Then he won to the full fruition
> Of that which he had seen in vision.

Half a century after his death, Thomas Halyburton, who was a successor to Rutherford as professor of divinity at St. Andrews, requested on his deathbed that he would be buried alongside his predecessor. On his last day of life he confessed, "I was just thinking of the pleasant plot of earth that I will get to lie in beside Mr. Rutherford, and Oh! we will be a knot of bonnie dust!

Chapter Four

THE SERAPHIC LETTERS

෴

Robert McWard published the first collection of Rutherford's letters in 1664, three years after the death of their author. Since then they have held a unique place, not only in the devotional literature of Scotland, but the whole of the Christian Church. The author Adam Philip D.D., declares "It would be impossible, except by reproducing the 'Letters' themselves, to give any adequate idea of their richness and wisdom. The troubled will find in them a well of consolation. Hearts that are longing for Christ will feel stirred and inflamed with a great glow. The whole circle of Christian life, its difficulties, its duties, its hopes, the heights and depths of faith and experience, everything that belongs to the Gospel and to its challenge, to holiness and its fruition, to the rightful recognition of God and to the understanding of the unsearchable riches of Christ, are spoken of with insight and passion and with a force that is compelling."

His eighteen month exile to Aberdeen, from August 1636 until February 1638, was accepted by him as a great honour 'bestowed upon him by his kind Lord.' "I go" he said, "to my King's palace of Aberdeen and tongue or pen or wit cannot express my joy."

Although he was forbidden to preach, he was allowed to write letters, and of the 365 which we possess, well over half of them were written from Aberdeen. It has been said by the Rev. Andrew Thompson that "His Master sent him into exile to write letters."

These letters not only reveal Rutherford's intimate communion with his beloved Lord, they are also rich in spiritual counsel and comfort, and are just as relevant today as they were three and a half centuries ago.

These extracts which I have chosen will I believe, justify the estimation of C. H. Spurgeon, who reckoned Rutherford's Letters to be 'the nearest thing to inspiration which can be found in all the writings of mere men.'

∽

The Furnace of Affliction

It is good for me that I have been afflicted. Psalm 119 v.71

"He was a Son of Consolation because he was himself a Son of Affliction. Every Life and notice of him tells of the relentless persecution and privations that he endured. It is a blessing for a minister or any worker for Christ to know personally the sorrows of his people, so as not to speak or write from the outside." Dr. A. B. Grosart

Know you not that Christ wooeth His wife in the furnace? "Behold I have refined thee, but not with silver; I have chosen thee in the furnace of affliction" He casteth His love on you when you are in the furnace of affliction. You might indeed be cast down if He brought you in and left you there; but when He leadeth you through the waters, think ye not that He has a sweet soft hand? You know His love grip already; you shall be delivered, wait on. Jesus will make a road, and come and fetch home the captive. Your winter night is near spent; it is near-hand the dawning. This wilderness shall bud and grow up like a rose.

It is good that your crosses will but convoy you to heaven's gates: in - they cannot go; the gates shall be closed upon them, when ye shall be admitted to the throne. Time standeth not still, eternity is hard at our door. Oh, what is laid up for you! Therefore, harden your face against the wind.

The thorn is one of the most cursed, and angry, and crabbed weeds that the earth yieldeth, and yet out of it springeth the rose, one of the sweetest-smelled flowers, and most delightful to the eye, that the earth hath. Your Lord shall make joy and gladness out of your afflictions; for all His roses have a fragrant smell. Wait for the time when His own holy hand shall hold them to your nose; and if ye would have present comfort under the cross, be much in prayer, for at that time your faith kisseth Christ and He kisseth the soul.

Every man thinketh he is rich enough in grace, till he take out his purse, and tell his money, and then he findeth his pack but poor and light in the day of a heavy trial. I found that I had not to bear my expenses, and I should have fainted, if want and penury had not chased me to the storehouse of all.

Venture through the thick of all things after Christ, and lose not your Master, Christ, in the throng of this great market. Let Christ know how heavy, and how many a stone-weight you and your cares, burdens, crosses, and sins are. Let Him bear all. ... And then, let the wind blow out of what airt it will, your soul shall not be blown into the sea.

Lay all your loads and your weights by faith upon Christ; take ease to yourself, and let Him bear all. I rejoice that He hath come, and hath chosen you in the furnace; it was even there where ye and He set tryst. That is an old gate of Christ's: He keepeth the good old fashion with you, that was in Hosea's days: "Therefore, behold, I will allure her, and bring her into the wilderness, and speak to her heart." There was no talking to her heart while He and she were in the fair and flourishing city, and at ease; but out in the cold, hungry, waste wilderness, He allured her, He whispered news into her ear there, and said, "Thou art Mine."

We fools would have a cross of our own choosing, and would have our gall and wormwood sugared, our fire cold, and our death and grave warmed with heat of life; but He who hath brought many children to glory, and lost none, is our best Tutor. I wish that, when I am sick, He may be keeper and comforter. But I know it is my softness and weakness; who would ever be ashore when a fit of seasickness cometh on; though I know I shall come soon enough to that desirable country, and shall not be displaced: none shall take my lodging.

Your afflictions are not eternal; time will end them, and so shall ye at length see the Lord's salvation, His love sleepeth not, but is still working for you. His salvation will not tarry nor linger; and suffering for Him is the noblest cross that is out of heaven, ... It is a love-look to heaven and the other side of the water that God seeketh; and this is the fruit, the flower and bloom growing out of your cross, that ye be a dead man to time, to clay, to gold, to country, to friends, wife, children, and all pieces of created things; for in them there is not a seat nor bottom for soul's love. Oh, what room is for your love (if it were as broad as the sea) up in heaven, and in God! And what would not Christ give for your love? God gave so much for your soul; and blessed are ye if ye have a "love for Him, and can call in your soul's love from all idols, and can make a God of God, a God of Christ, and draw a line betwixt your heart and Him. ...Let the Lord absolutely have the ordering of your evils and troubles; and put them off you by recommending your cross and your furnace to Him who hath skill to melt His own metal, and knoweth well what to do with His furnace. Let your heart be willing that God's fire have your tin, and brass, and dross. When ye are over the water, this case shall be a yesterday past a hundred years ere ye were born; and the cup of glory shall wash the memory of all this away, and make it as nothing. The Lord is rising up to do you good in the latter end; put on the faith of His salvation, and see Him posting and hasting towards you.

If your Lord calls you to suffering, be not dismayed; there shall be a new allowance of the King for you when you come to it. One of the softest pillows Christ hath is laid under His witnesses' head, though often they must set down their bare feet among thorns.

The worst things of Christ, His reproaches, His cross, are better than Egypt's treasures. He hath opened His door, and taken into His house-of-wine a poor sinner, and hath left me so sick of love for my Lord Jesus, that if heaven were at my disposing, I would give it for Christ, and would not be content to go to heaven, except I were persuaded that Christ were there.

I find that my extremity hath sharpened the edge of His love and kindness, so that He seemeth to devise new ways of expressing the sweetness of His love to my soul. Suffering for Christ is the very element wherein Christ's love liveth, and exerciseth itself. And if Christ weeping in sackcloth be so sweet, I cannot find any imaginable thoughts to think what He will be, when we clay-bodies (having put off mortality) shall come up to the marriage hall and great palace, and behold the King clothed in His royal robes, sitting on His throne. I would desire no more for my heaven beneath the moon, while I am sighing in this house of clay, but daily renewed feasts of love with Christ.

Sickness. Sure I am, it is better to be sick, providing Christ come to the bedside and draw by the curtains, and say, "Courage, I am thy salvation," than to enjoy health, being lusty and strong, and never to be visited of God.

Weakness. Oh, how sweet it is for a sinner to put his weakness into Christ's strengthening hand, and to father a sick soul upon such a Physician, and to lay weakness before Him to weep upon Him, and to plead and pray! Weakness can speak and cry, when we have not a tongue. " And when I passed by thee, and saw thee polluted in thy own blood, I said unto thee, when thou wast in thy blood, Live." …As for weakness, we have it that we may employ Christ's strength because of our weakness.

Chastening. Ye are His Wheat, growing in our Lord's field; and if wheat, ye must go under our Lord's threshing-instrument, in His barn floor, and through His sieve, and through His mill to be bruised... that ye may be found good bread in your Lord's house. I am persuaded your glass is spending itself by little and little; and if ye knew who is before you, ye would rejoice in your tribulations. Think ye it a small honour to stand before the throne of God and the Lamb? And to be clothed in white and called to the marriage supper of the Lamb? To be led to the fountain of living waters, and to come to the Well-head, even God Himself, and get your fill of the clear, cold, sweet, refreshing water of life, the King's own well?...Up your heart! Shout for joy! Your King is coming to fetch you to His Father's house.

O thrice fools are we, who, like newborn princes weeping in the cradle, know not that there is a kingdom before them! Then let our Lord's sweet hand square us and hammer us, and strike off the knots of pride, self-love, and world-worship, and infidelity, that He may make us stones and pillars in His Father's house.

It is the Lord's kindness that He will take the scum off us in the fire. Who knoweth how needful winnowing is to us, and what dross we must want ere we enter into the kingdom of God? So narrow is the entry to heaven, that our knots, our bunches and lumps of pride, and self-love, and idol-love, and world-love, must be hammered off us, that we may thring in, stooping low, and creeping through that narrow and thorny entry.

On this side of the New Jerusalem, we shall still have need of forgiving and healing grace. I find crosses of Christ's carved work that He marketh out for us, and that with crosses He figureth and portrayeth us to His own image, cutting away pieces of our ill and corruption. Lord cut, Lord carve, Lord wound, Lord do anything that may perfect Thy image in us, and make us meet for glory.

The World, the Flesh and the Devil

For all that is in the world, the lust of the flesh, and the lust of the eyes, and the pride of life, is not of the Father, but is of the world.
I John 2: 16

"These letters will ever be precious to all who are sensible of their own, and the Church's decay and corruptions – The wound and the cure are therein so fully opened out: self is exposed, specially spiritual self. He will tell you, 'There is as much need to watch over grace, as to watch over sin'. He will show you God in Christ, to fill up the place usurped by self. The subtleties of sin, idols, snares, temptations, self-deceptions, are dragged into view from time to time. And what is better still, the cords of Christ are twined round the roots of these bitter plants, that they may be plucked up." Rev. Andrew A. Bonar

Lusts. Pride of youth, vanity, lusts, idolizing of the world, and charming pleasures, take long to root them out. ... When the day of visitation cometh, and your old idols come weeping about you, ye will have much ado not to break your heart.

It is impossible that a man can take his lusts to heaven with him; such wares as these will not be welcome there. Oh, how loath are we to forego our packalds and burdens that hinder us to run our race with patience! It is no small work to displease and anger nature, that we may please God. Oh, if it be hard to win one foot, or half an inch, out of our own will, out of our own wit, out of our own ease and worldly lusts (and so to deny ourselves, and to say, " It is not I but Christ, not I but grace, not I but God's glory, not I but God's love constraining me, not I but the Lord's word, not I but Christ's commanding power as King in me!"), oh, what pains, and what a death is it to nature, to turn me, myself, my lust, my ease, my credit, over unto, "My Lord, my Saviour, my King, and my God, my Lord's will, my Lord's grace!" But, alas! That idol, that whorish creature, myself, is the master-idol we all bow to. What hurried Eve headlong upon the forbidden fruit, but that wretched thing 'herself'. What drew that brother-murderer to kill Abel? That wild 'himself'. What drove the old world on to corrupt their ways? Who, but themselves, and their own pleasure. What was the cause of Solomon's falling into idolatry and multiplying of strange wives? What, but himself, whom he would rather pleasure than God. What was the hook that took David and snared him first in adultery, but his self-lust; and then in murder, but his self-credit and self-honour. What led Peter on to deny his Lord? Was it not a piece of himself, and self love to a whole skin? What made Judas sell his Master for thirty pieces of money, but a piece of self-love, idolizing of avaricious self. What made Demas go off the way of the gospel, to embrace this present world? Even self love and love of gain for himself. Every man blameth the devil for his sins; but the great devil, the house-devil of every man, the house-devil that eateth and lieth in every man's bosom, is that idol that killeth all, 'himself'. Oh, blessed are they who can deny themselves, and put Christ in the room of themselves! Oh, would to the Lord that I had not a 'myself,' but Christ; nor a 'my lust', but Christ; nor a 'my ease', but Christ; nor a 'my honour' but Christ! O sweet word! "I live no more, but Christ liveth in me!" Oh, if every one would put away himself, his own self, his own ease, his own pleasure, his own credit, and his own twenty things, his own hundred things, which he setteth up as idols, above Christ!

It is impossible that your idol-sins and ye can go to heaven together; and that they who will not part with these can indeed, love Christ at the bottom, but only in word and show, which will not do the business.

Contention. I think not much of a cross when all the children of the house weep with me and for me; and to suffer when we enjoy the communion of saints is not much; but it is hard when saints rejoice in the suffering of saints, and redeemed ones hurt (yea, even go nigh to hate) redeemed ones. I confess I imagined there had no more been such an affliction on earth, or in the world, as that one elect angel should fight against another. The saints are not Christ: there is no misjudging in Him; there is much in us; and a doubt it is, if we shall have fully one heart till we shall enjoy one heaven. Our starlight hideth us from ourselves and hideth us from one another, and Christ from us all. But He will not be hidden from us. ...The King's spikenard, Christ's perfume, His apples of love, His ointments, even down in this lower house of clay, are a choice heaven. Oh! what then is the King in His own land, where there is such a throne, so many King's palaces, ten thousand thousands of crowns of glory that want heads yet to fill them? Oh, so much leisure as shall be there to sing! Oh, such a tree as groweth there in the midst of that Paradise, where the inhabitants sing eternally under its branches!

Slandering. The times would make any that love the Lord sick and faint, to consider how iniquity aboundeth, and how dull we are in observing sins in ourselves, and how quick-sighted to find them out in others. And yet very often, when we complain oft times, we are secretly slandering the Lord's work and wise government of the world, and raising a hard report of Him. "He is good, and doeth good," and all His ways are equal. Oh, we are little with God and do all without God! We sleep and wake without Him; we eat, we speak, we journey, we go about worldly business and our calling without God! And considering what deadness is upon the hearts of many, it were good that some did not pray without God, and preach and praise, and read and confer of God without God! It is universally complained of, that there is a strange deadness upon the land, and on the hearts of His people.

The devil. Since we must have a devil to trouble us, I love a raging devil best. Our Lord knoweth what sort of devil we have need of: it is best that Satan be in his own skin, and look like himself.

My Lord Jesus had a good eye that the tempter should not play foul play, and blow out Christ's candle. When He burnt the house, He saved His own goods. And I believe the devil and the persecuting world shall reap no fruit of me, but burnt ashes: for He will see to His own gold, and save that from being consumed with the fire, Oh, what owe I to the file, to the hammer, to the furnace of my Lord Jesus! Who hath now let me see how good the wheat of Christ is, that goeth through His mill, and His oven, to be made bread for His own table. Grace tried is better than grace, and it is more than grace; it is glory in its infancy.

Many make a start toward heaven who fall on their back, and win not up to the top of the mount. It plucketh heart and legs from them, and they sit down and give it over, because the devil setteth a sweet-smelled flower to their nose (this fair adorned world), wherewith they are bewitched, and so forget or refuse to go forward,

꩜

The House of Mourning

It is better to go to the house of mourning, than to go to the house of feasting: for that is the end of all men; and the living will lay it to his heart.   Ecclesiastes 7: 2

"Few men knew as Rutherford did how to interpret Providence by the Word, and the Word by Providence, which he sometimes described as marginal readings placed alongside of the inspired page.   How many a sorrowful countenance did he light up with a strange joy! Some of the most beautiful passages in his letters, or indeed in religious literature, were written to mothers at Anwoth when they had been bereaved of an only son. "   Rev. Dr. Andrew Thompson.

Faith will teach you to kiss a striking Lord; and so acknowledge the sovereignty of God (in the death of a child) to be above the power of us mortal men, who may pluck up a flower in the bud and not be blamed for it. If our dear Lord pluck up one of His roses, and pull down sour and green fruit before harvest, who can challenge Him? For He sendeth us to His world, as men to a market, wherein some stay many hours, and eat and drink, and buy and sell, and pass through the fair, till they be weary; and such are those who live long, and get a heavy fin of this life. And others again come slipping in to the morning market, and do neither sit nor stand, nor buy nor sell, but look about them a little, and pass presently home again; and these are infants and young ones, who end their short market in the morning, and get but a short view of the fair. Our Lord, who hath numbered man's months, and set him bounds that he cannot pass, hath written the length of our market, and it is easier to complain of the decree than to change it.

Believe that he is not gone away, but sent before; and that the change of the country should make you think that he is not lost to you who is found to Christ, and that he is now before you; and that the dead in Christ shall rise again. A going-down star is not annihilated, but shall appear again. If he hath cast his bloom and flower, the bloom is fallen in heaven, into Christ's lap. And as he was lent a while to time, so he is given now to eternity, which will take yourself. The difference of your shipping and his to heaven and Christ's shore, the land of life, is only in some few years, which weareth every day shorter; and some short and soon-reckoned summers will give you a meeting with him... If death were a sleep that had no wakening, we might sorrow.... He breweth your cup: therefore, drink it patiently and with the better will. Stay and wait on, till Christ loose the knot that fasteneth His cross on your back; for He is coming to deliver, and I pray you, learn to be worthy of His pains who correcteth. And let Him wring and be ye washen; for He hath a Father's heart, and a Father's hand, which is training you up, and making you meet for the high hall. This school of suffering is a preparation for the King's higher house; and let all your visitations speak all the letters of your Lord's summons. They cry –"O vain world!" "O bitter sin!" "O short and uncertain time!" "O fair eternity that is above sickness of death!" "O kingly and princely Bridegroom! Hasten glory's marriage, shorten time's short-spun and soon broken thread, and conquer sin!" ...And the Spirit and the Bride say, "Come!" and answer ye with them, "Even so, come, Lord Jesus! Come quickly!"

Think her not absent who is in such a Friend's house. Is she lost to you who is found to Christ? If she were with a dear friend, although you should never see her again, your care for her would be but small. Oh is she not now with a dear Friend and gone higher, upon a certain hope that ye shall, in the Resurrection, see her again. You would be sorry either to be, or to be esteemed, an atheist; and yet, not I, but the Apostle, thinketh those to be hopeless atheists who mourn excessively for the dead. Follow her, but envy her not; for indeed it is self-love in us that maketh us mourn for them that die in the Lord. Take heed then, that in showing your affection in mourning for your daughter, ye be not, out of self-affliction, mourning for yourself. ...Your daughter is plucked out of the fire, and she resteth from her labours; and your Lord, in that, is trying you, and casteth you in the fire. Go through all fire to your rest. While ye prodigally spend time in mourning for her, ye are speedingly posting after her. Run with patience your race. Let God have His own; and ask of Him, instead of your daughter which He hath taken from you, the daughter of faith, which is patience; and in patience possess your soul. Lift up your head: ye do not know how near your redemption doth draw!

As I have heard of the death of your daughter with heaviness of mind on your behalf, so am I much comforted that she hath evidenced to yourself and other witnesses the hope of the resurrection of the dead. Though we cannot outrun nor overtake them that are gone before, yet we shall quickly follow them; and the difference is, that she hath the advantage of some months or years of the crown before you and her mother. As we do not take it ill if our children outrun us in the life of grace, why then are we sad if they outstrip us in the attainment of the life of glory? It would seem that there is more reason to grieve that children live behind us, than that they are glorified and die before us. All the difference is in some poor hungry accidents of time, less or more, sooner or later. Ye would have lent her to glorify the Lord upon earth, and He hath borrowed her (with promise to restore her again) to be an organ of the immediate glorifying of Himself in heaven. Sinless glorifying of God is better than sinful glorifying of Him.

Dearest brother, go on and faint not. Something of yours is in heaven, beside your exalted Saviour; and ye go on after your own. Time's thread is shorter by one inch than it was. I make bold, in Christ, to speak my poor thoughts to you concerning your son lately fallen asleep in the Lord. I know that grace rooteth not out the affections of a mother, but putteth them upon His wheel who maketh all things new, that they may be refined: therefore, sorrow for a dead child is allowed to you, though by measure and ounce-weights. He commandeth you to weep: and that princely One, who took up to heaven with Him a man's heart to be a compassionate High Priest, became your fellow and companion on earth by weeping for the dead. The cup ye drink was at the lip of Jesus, and He drank of it; and I conceive ye love it not the worse that it is thus sugared. Therefore drink, and believe the resurrection of your son's body. The good Husbandman may pluck His roses, and gather His lilies at midsummer, and, for aught I dare say, in the beginning of the first summer month; and He may transplant young trees out of the lower ground to the higher, where they may have more of the sun, and a more free air, at any season of the year. What is that to you or me? The goods are His own. The Creator of time and winds did a merciful injury {if I dare borrow the word) to nature, in landing the passenger so early. They love the sea too well that complain of a fair wind, and a desirable tide, and a speedy coming ashore in that land where all the inhabitants have everlasting joy upon their heads.

Violent death is a sharer with Christ in His death, which was violent. It maketh not much what way we go to heaven: the happy home is all, where the roughness of the way shall be forgotten. He is gone home to a Friend's house, and made welcome, and the race is ended: time is recompensed with eternity, and copper with gold.

It hath seemed good, as I hear, to Him that hath appointed the bounds for the number of our months, to gather in a sheaf of ripe corn in the death of your Christian mother, into His garner. It is the more evident that winter is near, when apples, without the violence of wind, fall of their own accord off the tree. She is now above the winter, with a little change of place, not of a Saviour; only she enjoyeth Him now without messages, and in His own immediate presence, from whom she heard by letters and messengers before. I grant that death is to her a very new thing; but heaven was prepared of old. And Christ (as enjoyed in His highest throne, and as loaded with glory, and incomparably exalted above men and angels) is to her a new thing, but so new as the first summer-rose, or the first fruits of that heavenly field; or as a new paradise to a traveller, broken and worn out of breath with the sad occurrences of a long and dirty way. It cost her no more to go thither, than to suffer death to do her this piece of service: for by Him who was dead, and is alive, she was delivered from the second death. What, then, is the first death to the second? Not a scratch of the skin of a finger to the endless second death. And now she sitteth for eternity in a very considerable land, which hath more than four summers in the year. Oh, what springtime is there! What a singing life is there! There is not a dumb bird in all that large field; but all sing and breathe out heaven, joy, glory, dominion to the high Prince of that new found land. And verily, the land is the sweeter that Jesus Christ paid so dear a rent for it. And He is the glory of the land: all which, I hope, doth not so much mitigate and allay your grief for her part (though truly this should seem sufficient), as the unerring expectation of the dawning of that day upon yourself, and the hope that you have of the fruition of that same King and kingdom to your own soul.

If the place she hath left were any other than a prison of sin, and the home she is gone to any other than where her Head and Saviour is King of the land, your grief had been more rational. But I trust your faith of the resurrection of the dead in Christ to glory and immortality, will lead you to suspend your longing for her, till the morning and dawning of that day when the archangel shall descend with a shout, to gather all the prisoners out of the grave, up to Himself. To believe this is best for you; and to be silent, because He hath done it, is your wisdom.

It hath pleased the Lord to remove your husband soon to his rest; but shall we be sorry that our loss is his gain, seeing his Lord would want his company no longer? Think not much of short summons; for, seeing he walked with his Lord in his life, and desired that Christ should be magnified in him at his death, ye ought to be silent and satisfied. Know that the wounds of your Lord Jesus are the wounds of a lover, and that He will have compassion upon a sad-hearted servant; and that Christ hath said He will have the husband's room in your heart. He loved you in your first husband's time, and He is but wooing you still. Give Him heart and chair, house and all. He will not be made companion with any other. Love is full of jealousies:

He will have all your love; and who should get it but He? I know that ye allow it upon Him. There are comforts both sweet and satisfying laid up for you: wait on.

⌒

The Word of Comfort

These things have I spoken unto you, that in me ye might have peace. In the world ye shall have tribulation: but be of good cheer; I have overcome the world. *John 16: 33*

"What wealth of spiritual ravishment we have here! Rutherford is beyond all praise of men. Like a strong-winged eagle he soars unto the highest heaven and with unblenched eye he looks into the mystery of love divine. There is, to us, something mysterious, awe-creating and superhuman about Rutherford's letters." Rev. C. H. Spurgeon

Ye cannot, ye must not, have a more pleasant or more easy condition here, than He had, who through afflictions was made perfect. We may indeed think, "Cannot God bring us to heaven with ease and prosperity?" Who doubteth but He can? But His infinite wisdom thinketh and decrees the contrary; and we cannot see a reason for it, yet He hath a most just reason. We never with our eyes saw our own soul; yet we have a soul. We see many rivers, but we know not their first spring and original fountain; yet they have a beginning. When ye are come to the other side of the water, and have set down your foot on the shore of glorious eternity, and look back again to the waters and to your wearisome journey, and shall see, in that clear glass of endless glory, nearer to the bottom of God's wisdom, ye shall then be forced to say, "If God had done otherwise with me than He hath done, I had never come to the enjoying of this crown of glory." Whether God comes to His children with a rod or a crown, if He come Himself with it, it is well. Welcome, welcome, Jesus, what way soever Thou come, if we can get a sight of Thee.

Till He take His children out of the furnace that knoweth how long they should be tried, there is no deliverance; but after God's highest and fullest tide, when the sea of trouble is gone over the souls of His children, then comes the gracious long-hoped-for ebbing and drying up of the waters. Do not faint; the wicked may hold the bitter cup to your head, but God mixeth it, and there is no poison in it. They strike, but God moves the rod; Shimei curseth, but it is because the Lord bids him.

Ere it be long, our Master will be at us, and bring this whole world out, before the sun and daylight, in their blacks and whites. Happy are they who are found watching. Our sand glass is not so long as we need to weary; time will eat away and root out our woes and sorrow. Our heaven is in the bud, and growing up to a harvest. Why, then, should we not follow on, seeing that our span-length of time will come to an inch? Therefore I commend Christ to you, as the staff of your old age. Let Him now have the rest of your days. And think not much of a storm upon the ship that Christ saileth in: there shall no passenger fall overboard, but the crazed ship and the seasick passenger shall come to land safe,

I long to know how matters stand betwixt Christ and your soul. I know that ye find Him still the longer the better: time cannot change Him in His love. Ye may yourself ebb and flow, rise and fall, wax and wane; but your Lord is this day as He was yesterday. And it is your comfort that your salvation is not rolled upon wheels of your own making, neither have ye to do with a Christ of your own shaping. God hath singled out a Mediator strong and mighty: if ye and your burdens were as heavy as ten hills or hells, He is able to bear you, and save you to the uttermost. Your often seeking to Him cannot make you a burden to Him. I know that Christ compassionateth you, and maketh a moan for you, in all your dumps, and under your down castings; but it is good for you that He hideth Himself sometimes. It is not niceness, dryness, nor coldness of love that causeth Christ to withdraw, that ye cannot see Him; but He knoweth that ye could not bear with up sails, a fair gale, a full moon, and a high spring tide of His felt love, and always a fair summer day and a summer sun of a felt and possessed and embracing Lord Jesus. He could not let out

His rivers of love upon His own, but these rivers would be in hazard of loosening a young plant at the root. Ye should, therefore, frist (put off for a time) Christ's kindness, as to its sensible and full manifestations, till ye and He be above sun and moon. That is the country where ye will be enlarged for that love which ye dow (can) not now contain. Lighten your heart by laying your all upon Him.

Faint not, because this world and ye are at yea and nay, and because this is not a home that laugheth upon you. The wise Lord, who knoweth you, will have it so, because He casteth a net for your love, to catch it and gather it in to Himself. Therefore, bear patiently the loss of children, and burdens, and other discontentments, either within or without the house: your Lord in them is seeking you, and seek ye Him. Let none be your love and choice, and the flower of your delights, but your Lord Jesus. Set not your heart upon the world, since God hath not made it your portion; for it will not fall to you to get two portions, and to rejoice twice, and to be happy twice, and to have an upper heaven, and an under heaven too.

Weary not, but come in and see if there be not more in Christ than the tongue of men and angels can express. If ye seek a gate to heaven, the way is in Him, or He is it. What ye want is treasured up in Jesus; and He saith all His are yours.

Your life is hid with Christ in God, and therefore ye cannot be robbed of it. Our Lord handleth us, as fathers do their young children; they lay up jewels in a place, above the reach of the short arms of bairns, else bairns would put up their hands and take them down, and lose them soon. So hath our Lord done with our spiritual life. Jesus Christ is the high coffer in which our Lord hath hid our life; we children are not able to reach up our arm so high as to take down that life and lose it; it is in our Christ's hand. So long as this life is not hurt, all other troubles are but touches in the heel.

Let us not weary: the miles to that land are fewer and shorter than when we first believed. Strangers are not wise to quarrel with their host, and complain of their lodging. It is a foul way but a fair home.

The hope of it in the end is a heart some convoy in the way.

The saints know not the length and largeness of the sweet earnest, and of the sweet green sheaves before the harvest, that might be had on this side of the water, if we would take more pains. We all go to heaven with less earnest, and lighter purses of the hoped for sum, than otherwise we might do, if we took more pains to win further in upon Christ, in this pilgrimage of our absence from Him.

Oh that every hair of my head, and every member and every bone in my body, was a man to witness a fair confession for Him! I would think all too little for Him. When I look over beyond the line, and beyond death, to the laughing side of the world, I triumph, and ride upon the high places of Jacob; howbeit otherwise I am faint, dead hearted, cowardly man, oft borne down and hungry in waiting for the marriage supper of the Lamb. Nevertheless, I think it the Lord's wise love that feeds us with hunger, and makes us fat with wants and desertions.

We are fallen in winnowing and trying times. I am glad that your breath serveth you to run to the end, in the same condition and way wherein ye have walked these twenty years past. It is either the way of peace, or we are yet in our sins, and have missed the way! The Lord, it is true, hath stained the pride of all our glory; and now, last of all, the sun hath gone down upon many of the prophets. But stumble not; men are but men, and God appeareth more and more to be God, and Christ is still Christ. A stronger than I am had almost stumbled me and cast me down. But oh what mercy it is to discern between what is Christ's and what is man's, and what way the hue, colour, and lustre of gifts of grace dazzle and deceive our weak eyes! Oh to be dead to all things that are below Christ, were it even a created heaven and created grace! Holiness is not Christ; nor are the blossoms and flowers of the Tree of Life the tree itself. Men and creatures may wind themselves between us and Christ; and, therefore, the Lord hath done much to take out of the way all betwixt Him and us. The fairest things, and most eminent in Britain, are stained, and have lost their lustre; only Christ keepeth His greenness and beauty, and remaineth what He was. Oh, if He were more and more excellent to our apprehensions than ever He was (whose excellency is above all apprehensions), and still more and more sweet to our taste! I care for nothing, if so be that I were nearer to Him. And yet He fleeth not from me: I flee from Him, but He pursueth.

Make you ready to meet the Lord; and rest and sleep in the love of that Fairest among the sons of men. Desire Christ's beauty. Give out all your love to Him, and let none fall by. Learn in prayer to speak to Him.

The Lord hath told you what ye should be doing till He come. "Wait and hasten," saith Peter, "for the coming of our Lord." All is night that is here, in respect of ignorance and daily ensuing troubles, one always making way to another, as the ninth wave of the sea to the tenth; therefore sigh and long for the dawning of that morning, and the breaking of that day of the coming of the Son of Man, when the shadows shall flee away. Persuade yourself the King is coming; read His letter sent before Him, "Behold, I come quickly." Wait with the wearied night-watch for the breaking of the eastern sky, and think that ye have not a morrow. As the wise father said, who, being invited against to-morrow to dine with his friend, answered, "These many days I have had no morrow at all."

∞

The Way of the Cross

But God forbid that I should glory, save in the cross of our Lord Jesus Christ, by whom the world is crucified unto me, and I unto the world.   Galatians 6: 14

"It was his superb power to set Christ before men in moral splendour and saving goodness that made him great as an exponent of His Crown and Covenant." Rev. Dr. Marcus L. Loane

Sweet, sweet is His cross; light, light, and easy is His yoke. O what a sweet step were it up to my Father's house through ten deaths, for the truth and cause of that unknown, and so not half well-loved, Plant of Renown, the Man called the Branch, the Chief among ten thousand, the Fairest among the sons of men. O what unseen joys, how many hidden heart-burnings of love are in the remnants of the sufferings of Christ! Welcome, welcome, sweet, sweet and glorious cross of Christ; welcome, sweet Jesus, with Thy light cross; Thou hast now gained and gotten all my love from me; keep what Thou hast gotten.

Take his cross with him cheerfully. Christ and His cross are not separable in this life; howbeit, Christ and His cross part at heaven's door, *for there is no houseroom for crosses in heaven.* One tear, one sigh, one sad heart, one fear, one loss, one thought of trouble, cannot find lodging there; they are but the marks of our Lord Jesus down in this wide inn, and stormy country on this side of death: *sorrow and the saints are not married together* or, suppose it were so, Heaven would make a divorce.

How sad a prisoner should I be if I knew not that my Lord Jesus had the keys of the prison Himself, and that His death and blood have bought a blessing to our crosses as well as to ourselves! I am sure that troubles have no prevailing right over us, if they be but our Lord's sergeants, to keep us in ward while we are in this side of heaven. I am persuaded, also, that they shall not go over the boundary-line, nor enter into heaven with us; for they find no welcome there, where "there is no more death, neither sorrow, nor crying, neither any more pain;" and, therefore, we shall leave them behind us.

I find one thing which I saw not well before: that when the saints are under trials and well humbled, little sins raise great cries and war-shouts in the conscience, and in prosperity conscience is a Pope, to give dispensations, and let out and in, and give latitude and elbow room to the heart. O, how little care we for pardon at Christ's hand when we make dispensations! And all is but child's play till a cross without begets a heavier cross within, and then we play no longer with our idols. It is good still to be severe against ourselves, for we but transform God's mercy into an idol, and an idol that hath a dispensation to give for the turning of the grace of God into wantonness.

Your Lord hath the pick and choice of ten thousand other crosses besides this, to exercise you withal; but His wisdom and His love selected and chose out this for you besides them all; and take it as a choice one and make use of it, so as you look to this world as your stepmother in your borrowed prison. For it is a love-look to heaven and the other side of the water that God seeketh; and this is the fruit, the flower and bloom growing out of your cross, that you be a dead man to time, to clay, to gold, to country, to friends, wife, children, and all pieces of created nothings; for in them is not a seat nor bottom for soul's love.

When His people cannot have a providence of silk and roses, they must be content with such an one as He carveth out for them. You would not go to heaven but with company; and you may perceive that the way of those who went before you was through blood, sufferings, and many afflictions: nay, Christ, the Captain, went in over the door-threshold of Paradise, bleeding to death. I do not think but you have learned to stoop, and that you have found that the apples and sweet fruits which grow on that crabbed tree of the cross are as sweet as it is sour to bear it; especially considering that Christ hath borne the whole complete cross, and that His saints bear but bits and chips; as the Apostle says, "the remnants, or bearings of the cross."

I have but small experience of suffering for Him; but let my Judge and Witness in heaven lay my soul in the balance of justice, if I find not a young heaven, a little paradise of glorious comforts and soul-delighting love kisses of Christ here beneath the moon, in suffering for Him and His truth; and that the glory, joy, and peace, and fire of love, which I thought had been kept until supper-time, when we shall get leisure to feast our fill upon Christ, I have felt in glorious beginnings in my bonds for this princely Lord Jesus.

Our sufferings are washed in Christ's blood, as well as our souls;

for Christ's merits brought a blessing to the crosses of the sons of God. We are over the water some way already; we are married, and our marriage portion is paid; we are already more than conquerors, "as dying, and behold we live." I never before heard of a living death, or a quick death, but ours: our death is not like the common death; Christ's skill, His handiwork, and a new cast of Christ's admirable act, may be seen in our quick death. I bless the Lord that all our troubles come through Christ's fingers, and that He casteth sugar among them, and casteth in some ounce weights of Heaven, and of the spirit of glory, that resteth on suffering believers, into one cup, in which there is no taste of hell.

If you go to weigh Jesus, His sweetness, excellency, glory, and beauty, and lay opposite to Him your ounces, or drachms of suffering for Him, you will be straitened in two ways:

1. It will be a pain to make the comparison, the disproportion being by no understanding imaginable; nay, if Heaven's arithmetic and angels were set to work, they should never number the degrees of difference.

2. It would straiten you to find a scale for the balance to lay that high and lofty One, that over-transcending Prince of Excellency in. If your mind could fancy as many created heavens as time hath had minutes, trees have had leaves, and clouds have had rain-drops, since the first stone of the creation was laid, they would not make half a scale in which to bear and weigh boundless excellency.

Men have no more of you to work upon than some inches and span-lengths of sick, coughing, and phlegmatic clay. Your souls, your love to Christ, your faith, cannot be summoned, nor sentenced, nor accused, nor condemned by Pope, deputy, prelate, ruler, or tyrant. Your faith is a free lord, and cannot be a captive. All the malice of hell and earth can but hurt the scabbard of a believer; and death, at the most, can get but a clay-pawn in keeping till your Lord takes the king's keys, and opens your graves.

∞

The Excellencies of Christ

And the word was made flesh, and dwelt among us, (and we beheld his glory, the glory as of the only begotten of the Father,) full of grace and truth. John 1:14

"Nothing is more needed in our day in the Christian Church than a larger sight, by faith, of 'the King in His beauty.' We hear much of many things, but too little of Him. To read Rutherford, in sympathy and with prayer, is a powerful and beautiful help towards that 'beatific vision' of our Redeemer which may be ours even here below."   Handley Dunelm, Bishop of Durham.

Christ and His fullness. Who knoweth how far it is to the bottom of our Christ's fullness, and to the ground of our heaven? Who ever weighed Christ in a pair of balances? Who hath seen the folding and plies, and the heights and depths of that glory which is in Him, and kept for us?

He is every way higher, and deeper, and broader than the shallow and ebb hand breadth of my short and dim light can take up; and, therefore, I would that my heart could be silent, and sit down in the learnedly ignorant wondering at the Lord, whom men and angels cannot comprehend. I know that the noonday light of the highest angels, who see Him face to face, sees not the borders of His infiniteness. They apprehend God near hand; but they cannot comprehend Him. Oh, let this bit of love of ours, this inch and half-span length of heavenly longing, meet with Thy infinite Love! Oh, if the little I have were swallowed up with the infiniteness of that excellency which is in Christ! Our wants should soon be swallowed up with His fullness.

Christ and His Excellencies. " Come and see " maketh Christ to be known in His excellency and glory. It is little to see Christ in a book, as men do the world in a card. They talk of Christ by the book and the tongue, and no more; but to come nigh Christ, and salute Him, and embrace Him, is another thing.

Look into those depths (without a bottom) of loveliness, sweetness, beauty, excellency, glory, goodness, grace, and mercy, that are in Christ; and ye shall then cry down the whole world, and all the glory of it, even when it is come to the summer-bloom; and ye shall cry, "Up with Christ, up with Christ's Father, up with eternity of glory!"

Christ and His love. His love hath neither brim nor bottom; His love is like Himself, it passeth all natural understanding. I go to fathom it with my arms; but it is as if a child would take the globe of sea and land in his two short arms.

They are happy evermore who are over head and ears in the love of Christ, and know no sickness but love-sickness for Christ, and feel no pain but the pain of an absent and hidden Well-Beloved. We run our souls out of breath and tire them, in coursing and galloping after our night-dreams (such are the rovings of our miscarrying hearts), to get some created good thing in this life, and on this side of death. We would fain stay and spin out a heaven to ourselves, on this side of the water; but sorrow, want, changes, crosses, and sin are both woof and warp in that ill-spun web. Oh, how sweet and dear are those thoughts that are still upon the things that are above! And how happy are they who are longing to have little sand in their glass, and to have time's thread cut, and can cry to Christ, "Lord Jesus, have over; come and fetch the dreary passenger!" I wish that our thoughts were more frequently upon our country than they are. Oh, but heaven casteth a sweet smell afar off to those who have spiritual smelling! God hath made many fair flowers; but the fairest of them all is heaven, and the Flower of all flowers is Christ. Alas, that there is such a scarcity of love, and of lovers to Christ, amongst us all! Fly, fly, upon us, who love fair things, as fair gold, fair houses, fair lands, fair pleasures, fair honours, and fair persons, and do not pine and melt away with love to Christ! If those frothy, fluctuating, and restless hearts of ours would come all about Christ, and look into His love, to bottomless love, to the depth of mercy, to the unsearchable riches of His grace, to inquire after and search into the beauty of God in Christ, they would be swallowed up in the depth and height, length and breadth of His goodness. God send me no more, for my part of paradise, but Christ: and surely I were rich enough, and as well heavened as the best of them, if Christ were my heaven.

Hiding of His face is wise love. His love is not fond, doating, and reasonless. Nay, His bairns must often have the frosty cold side of the hill, and set down both their bare feet among the thorns. His love hath eyes, and in the meantime, is looking on. Our pride must have winter weather to rot it. The seasick passenger shall come to land; Christ will be the first to meet you on the shore. Keep the King's highway. Go on (in the strength of the Lord), in haste, as if ye had not leisure to speak to the innkeepers by the way. He is over beyond time, on the other side of the water, who thinketh long for you.

Would to God that all cold-blooded, faint-hearted soldiers of Christ would look again to Jesus, and to His love; and when they look, I would have them to look again and again, and fill themselves with beholding of Christ's beauty; and I dare say then that Christ would come into great court and request with many. But when I have spoken of Him, till my head rive, I have said just nothing. Set ten thousand thousand new-made worlds of angels and elect men, and double them in number, ten thousand, thousand, thousand times; let their heart and tongues be ten thousand thousand times more agile and large than the heart and tongues of the seraphim that stand with six wings before Him. When they have said all for the glorifying and praising of the Lord Jesus, they have but spoken little or nothing; His love will abide all possible creatures' praise. I am confounded with His incomparable love, and that He doth so great things for my soul, and hath got never yet anything of me worth the speaking of.

Running-over love (that vast, huge, boundless love of Christ) is the only thing I most fain would be in hands with. He knoweth that I have little but the love of that love; and that I shall be happy, suppose I never get another heaven but only an eternal, lasting feast of that love. But suppose my wishes were poor, He is not poor: Christ, all the seasons of the year, is dropping sweetness. If I had vessels, I might fill them; but my old, riven, and running-out dish, even when I am at the Well, can bring little away. Nothing but glory will make tight and fast our leaking and rifty vessels.

I want nothing but ways of expressing Christ's love. A full vessel would have a vent. Oh! It is a pity that there were not many imprisoned for Christ, were it for no other purpose than to write books and love-songs of the love of Christ. This love would keep all created tongues of men and angels in exercise, and busy night and day to speak of it. Alas! I can speak nothing of it, but wonder at three things in His love: First, freedom. O that lumps of sin should get such love for nothing! Secondly, the sweetness of His love. I give over either to speak or write of it; but those that feel it, may better bear witness what it is. But it is so sweet, that, next to Christ Himself, nothing can match it. And thirdly, what power and strength are in His love! It can climb a steep hill; and swim through water and not drown; and sing in the fire and find no pain; and triumph in losses, prisons, sorrows, exile, disgrace, and laugh and rejoice in death. Oh, when will we get our day, and heart's fill of that love! O time, time! How dost thou torment the souls of those that would be swallowed up of Christ's love, because thou movest so slowly! I know it is far after noon, and nigh the marriage-supper of the Lamb; the table is covered already. O Well-Beloved, run, run fast! O fair day, when wilt thou dawn! O shadows, flee away!

Oh, that our souls would so fall at odds with the love of this world, as to think of it as a traveller doth of a drink of water, which is not any part of his treasure, but goeth away with the using! For ten miles' journey maketh that drink to him as nothing. Oh, that we had as soon done with this world, and could as quickly dispatch the love of it! But as a child cannot hold two apples in his little hand, but the one putteth the other out of its room, so neither can we be masters and lords of two loves. Blessed were we, if we could make ourselves master of that invaluable treasure, the love of Christ; or rather suffer ourselves to be mastered and subdued to Christ's love, so as Christ were our "all things," and all other things our nothings, and the refuse of our delights.

His love came upon a withered creature, whether I would or not; and yet by coming it procured from me a welcome. A heart of iron, and iron doors, will not hold Christ out. I give Him leave to break iron locks and come in, and that is all.

My prayer to our Lord is, that ye may be sick of love for Him, who died of love for you, - I mean your Saviour Jesus. And O sweet were that sickness to be soul-sick for Him!

Christ, the Same.   Jesus, who upon earth ate and drank with publicans and sinners, and spake with harlots, and put up His holy hand and touched the leper's filthy skin, and came evermore nigh sinners, even now in glory, is yet the same Lord. His honour and His great court in heaven hath not made Him forget His poor friends on earth. In Him honours change not manners, and He doth yet desire your company.

Christ-Himself. Our love to Him should begin on earth, as it shall be in heaven; for the bride taketh not, by a thousand degrees, so much delight in her wedding garment as she doth in her bridegroom; so we, in the life to come, howbeit clothed with glory as with a robe, shall not be so much affected with the glory that goeth about us, as with the Bridegroom's joyful face and presence.

Christ beyond compare. Keep your first love with Jesus, fairer than all the children of men, There is none like Him; I would not exchange one smile of His lovely face with kingdoms. Let others take their silly, feckless heaven in this life. Envy them not; but let your soul, cast at all things and disdain them, except one only: either Christ or nothing.

Oh, what price can be given for Him? Angels cannot weigh Him. Oh, His weight, His worth, His sweetness, His overpassing beauty! If men and angels would come and look to that great and princely One, their ebbness could never take up His depth, their narrowness could never comprehend His breadth, height, and length. If ten thousand worlds of angels were created, they might all tire themselves in wondering at His beauty, and begin again to wonder.

O consider His loveliness and beauty, and that there is nothing which can commend and make fair heaven, or earth, or the creature, that is not in Him in infinite perfection; for fair sun and fair moon are black, and think shame to shine upon His fairness (Isaiah 24: 23). Be homely, and hunger for a feast and fill of His love; for that is the borders and march of heaven. Nothing hath a nearer resemblance to the colour, and hue, and lustre of heaven than Christ loved, and to breathe out love-words and love-sighs for Him. Remember what He is. When twenty thousand millions of heaven's lovers have worn their hearts threadbare of love, all is nothing, yea - less than nothing, to His matchless worth and excellency. Oh, so broad and so deep as the sea of His desirable loveliness is! Glorified spirits, triumphing angels, the crowned and exalted lovers of heaven, stand without His loveliness, and cannot put a circle on it. I but spill and lose words in speaking highly of Him who will bide and be above the music and songs of heaven, and never be enough praised by us all.

The discourses of angels, or love-books written by the congregation of seraphim (all their wits being conjoined and melted into one), would forever be in the nether side of truth, and of plentifully declaring the thing as it is. The infiniteness, the boundlessness of that incomparable excellency that is in Jesus, is a great word.

If I had as many angels' tongues as there have fallen drops of rain since the creation, or as there are leaves of trees in all the forests of the earth, or stars in the heaven, to praise, yet my Lord Jesus would ever be behind with me.

Put the beauty of ten thousand thousand worlds of paradises, like the garden of Eden, in one; put all trees, all flowers, all smells, all colours, all tastes, all joys, all sweetness, all loveliness, in one: oh, what a fair and excellent thing would that be! And yet it would be less to that fair and dearest Well-Beloved Christ, than one drop of rain to the whole seas, rivers, lakes, and fountains of ten thousand earths. Oh, but Christ is heaven's wonder, and earth's wonder! What marvel that His bride saith, "He is altogether lovely!"

Chapter Five

THE SANDS OF TIME ARE SINKING

∽

This well-known hymn was written by Mrs. Anne Ross Cousin of Melrose, Scotland and was first published in The Christian Treasury in 1857.

Anne the only daughter of Dr. David Ross Cundell of Leith, Scotland, was born in 1824. After her father's death when she was just three years of age, her family moved to Edinburgh and at the age of twenty-one she married the Rev. William Cousin, a Free Church minister in the town of Melrose, who was described as 'an honoured clergyman of the Free Church of Scotland.'

Although totally involved in her husband's work, Anne still found time to compose many beautiful hymns and poems. In 1876 a volume was published entitled *Immanuel's Land and Other Pieces*. This was a collection of one hundred and seven poems of which two in particular are still being sung today. They are *The **Substitute*** (Oh, Christ, what burdens bowed thy head) and ***Immanuel's Land*** (The sands of time are sinking).

Throughout her life, Anne loved to read 'The Life and Letters of Samuel Rutherford' and this was her inspiration for ***The Sands of***

Time are Sinking. It was composed in 1856 while she and her husband were ministering in Irvine, Scotland. In its original it consisted of nineteen verses and in 1857 the *Christian Treasury* published it in its entirety. Throughout the hymn she employs many phrases and similes from Rutherford's famous letters and indeed the title, *Immanuel's Land* is founded on the words of Rutherford as he lay on his deathbed "Oh, that all my brethren in the land may know what a Master I have served, and what peace I have this day! I shall sleep in Christ, and when I awake, I shall be satisfied with His likeness. This night shall close the door, and put my anchor within the veil; and I shall go away in a sleep by five of the clock in the morning. Glory, glory to my Creator and my Redeemer forever! I shall live and adore Him. Oh, for arms to embrace Him! Oh, for a well tuned harp. Glory, glory dwelleth in Immanuel's Land."

Just as he had predicted, Rutherford did indeed fall asleep in Christ at five o'clock that fair sweet morn, and awakened to a new dwelling place "in Immanuel's land."

It has been said "Rutherford is as the miner who found and furnished the gems, while Mrs. Cousin was as the skilful jeweller who sorted and arranged them into a chaplet for the king."

Mrs Cousin survived her husband by twenty-three years and for her 'The dawn of Heaven' broke on December 6th 1906. This hymn is the product of these two saintly servants of God and is the fruit of a long and loving study of the life and letters of Samuel Rutherford. Each verse makes reference to one or more of his sayings, and a selection of the more suitable verses appear in several hymnbooks today.

<blockquote>
The sands of time are sinking,
The dawn of Heaven breaks,
The summer morn I've sighed for,
The fair sweet morn awakes:
Dark, dark hath been the midnight,
But dayspring is at hand,
And glory, glory dwelleth
In Immanuel's land.
</blockquote>

Oh! well it is for ever,
Oh! well for evermore,
My nest hung in no forest
Of all this death-doomed shore:
Yes, let the vain world vanish,
As from the ship the strand,
While glory, glory dwelleth
In Immanuel's land.

There the Red Rose of Sharon
Unfolds its heart some bloom,
And fills the air in Heaven
With ravishing perfume:
Oh! to behold it blossom,
While by its fragrance fann'd
Where glory, glory dwelleth
In Immanuel's land.

The King there in His beauty,
Without a veil, is seen:
It were a well spent journey,
Though seven deaths lay between.
The Lamb, with His fair army,
Doth on Mount Zion stand,
And glory, glory dwelleth
In Immanuel's land.

Oh! Christ He is the Fountain,
The deep sweet well of love!
The *streams* on earth I've tasted,
More deep I'll drink above:
There, to ocean fullness,
His mercy doth expand,
And glory, glory dwelleth
In Immanuel's land.

E'en Anwoth was not heaven
E'en preaching was not Christ;
And in my sea-beat prison
My Lord and I held tryst:
And aye my murkiest storm cloud
Was by a rainbow spann'd,
Caught from the glory dwelling
In Immanuel's land.

But that He built a heaven
Of His surpassing love,
A little New Jerusalem,
Like to the one above,
"Lord, take me o'er the water,"
Had been my loud demand,
"Take me to love's own country,
Unto Immanuel's land.

But flowers need night's cool darkness
The moonlight and the dew;
So Christ, from one who loved it,
His shining oft withdrew;
And then for cause of absence,
My troubled soul I scanned
But glory, shadeless, shineth
In Immanuel's land.

The little birds of Anwoth
I used to count them blest,
Now, beside happier altars
I go to build my nest:
O'er these there broods no silence,
No graves around them stand,
For glory, deathless, dwelleth
In Immanuel's land.

Fair Anwoth by the Solway,
To me thou still art dear!
E'en from the verge of Heaven
I drop for thee a tear.
Oh! if one soul from Anwoth
Meet me at God's right hand,
My Heaven will be two Heavens,
In Immanuel's land.

I have wrestled on towards Heaven,
'Gainst storm, and wind, and tide,
Now, like a weary traveller,
That leaneth on his guide,
Amid the shades of evening,
While sinks life's ling' ring sand,
I hail the glory dawning
From Immanuel's land.

Deep waters crossed life's pathway,
The hedge of thorns was sharp;
Now these lie all behind me
Oh! for a well tuned harp!
Oh! to join halleluiah
With yon triumphant band,
Who sing, where glory dwelleth,
In Immanuel's land.

With mercy and with judgement
My web of time He wove,
And aye the dews of sorrow
Were lustred with His love.
I'll bless the hand that guided,
I'll bless the heart that planned,
When throned where glory dwelleth
In Immanuel's land.

Soon shall the cup of glory
Wash down earth's bitterest woes,
Soon shall the desert briar
Break into Eden's rose:
The curse shall change to blessing
The name on earth that's banned,
Be graven on the white stone
In Immanuel's land.

Oh! I am my Beloved's,
And my Beloved is mine!
He brings a poor vile sinner
Into His 'House of wine.'
I stand upon His merit,
I know no other stand,
Not e'en where glory dwelleth
In Immanuel's land.

I shall sleep sound in Jesus,
Filled with His likeness rise,
To live and to adore Him,
To see Him with these eyes.
'Tween me and resurrection
But Paradise doth stand;
Then, then for glory dwelling
In Immanuel's land.

The Bride eyes not her garment,
But her dear Bridegroom's face;
I will not gaze at glory,
But on my King of Grace,
Not at the crown he gifteth,
But on His pierced Hand:
The *Lamb* is all the glory
Of Immanuel's land.

I have borne scorn and hatred,
I have borne wrong and shame,
Earth's proud ones have reproached me,
For Christ's thrice blessed name:
Where God His seal set fairest
They've stamped their foulest brand;
But judgement shines like noonday
In Immanuel's land.

They've summoned me before them,
But there I may not come,
My Lord says, "Come up hither,"
My Lord says, "Welcome Home!"
My kingly King at His white throne,
My presence doth command,
Where glory, glory dwelleth
In Immanuel's land.

Chapter Six

QUAINT SERMONS OF SAMUEL RUTHERFORD

᠗

'One of the most moving and affectionate preachers in his time, or perhaps in any age of the church.' Robert Wodrow

Judged by any standard, Samuel Rutherford was a puritan divine, of outstanding eminence both as a theologian and pastor. A neighbouring minister, James Urqhart of Kinloss, said of him; "For such a piece of clay as Mr. Rutherford, I never knew one in Scotland like him. He seemed to be always praying, always preaching, always visiting the sick, always teaching in the schools, always writing treatises, always reading and studying."

Dr. Andrew Bonar said of his sermons; "He never fails to set Christ on high, for truly he had –

"A thirst no earthly stream could satisfy
A hunger that *must feed on Christ,* or die."

His life and ministry epitomised the words of Paul, 'For to me to live is Christ and to die is gain'. "Since he hath looked upon me," he wrote to one of his correspondents, "my heart is not mine own. He hath run away to heaven with it."

The majesty and loveliness of Christ was undoubtedly the main theme of both his letters and his sermons. Consider the note struck in the following quotations; "Everyday," he declares, "we see some new thing in Christ. His love hath neither brim nor bottom." "Look upon Him and love Him. Oh love and live." "Christ's love is young glory and young heaven."

As a faithful pastor he shunned not to declare the whole counsel of God. He was also careful to maintain a balance as he preached the doctrines of grace and other great truths relevant to godly living. He spoke to his congregation in a simple, quaint, compelling and imaginative manner, which resulted in the spiritual awakening of his church and the salvation of the lost.

One can imagine the effect upon his listeners of such words as these, taken from a Communion address. 'Mount Calvary, since God laid the first stone of it, did never bear such a weight as when the Lord of Glory was hanging upon a tree there. O! it was made a fair tree when such an Apple grew on it! It was a green orchard! It was our summer, but death's winter! Darkness was in all Judea when our Lord suffered. And why? Because the Candle that lighted the sun and the moon was blown out. The Godhead was eclipsed; and the world's eye was put out. He took away the sun with Him, as it were, to another world, when He that was the world's sun was put out. When He went out of the earth, the sun would not stay behind Him. Sun, what ails thee? "I have not will to shine when my Lord is going to another world." As if the sun had said to Jesus, "Lord, if Thou be going to another world, take me with You." The dead come out of the grave to welcome Christ's death. Life itself was coming to the grave, and therefore the graves opened, the dead lived; the bairns sprang and started in their mother's belly. Why? Because the Lord of Life was coming to the grave. The dead wondered, to see Life coming down among them. He went before hand, to sponge death and corruption for you.

"The warm devotion of the writer of the Letters," says Principal John Macleod, "went hand in hand with the scholastic passion for definition and discussion so that in one person he seemed to combine more persons than one in a multiple personality. He was the keen schoolman, the seraphic preacher, the patient pastor, the diligent catechist, the militant Churchman and the mystical man of God all in one."

∞

CHRIST'S NAPKIN

And God shall wipe away all tears from their eyes.
Revelation 21: 4 - 7.

A sermon preached at the Communion in Kirkcudbright,
May 12th 1633.

This title was no doubt given by the friend who took down the notes, for Rutherford was not in the way of putting titles to his sermons. The expression, *"Christ's Napkin,"* occurs in this sermon, and also in the sermon on John 20:13, which might as suitably be so called. The Edinburgh edition of 1734 says, *"By that flower of the Church, famous, famous Mr. Samuel Rutherford."*

This text contains four things. First: The state of the glorified in verse 4. Secondly: A part of Christ's office in verse 5. Thirdly: A description of His nature. Fourthly: The promises as to (1). Drink to satisfy the thirst; (2). An inheritance to the overcomers, or overcoming soldiers; (3). A threatening of eternal wrath to offenders against the first and second tables of the law.

"And God shall wipe away all tears."- When friends meet, they give the stranger his welcome-home. Here is the pilgrim's welcome that our friend, Christ, gives us. It was spoken from heaven, and therefore it is true doctrine. Then we see that the sufferings and tears of the saints shall be wiped away and removed, but not fully, until the world to come; for then is Christ's welcome-home to poor sinners. They come all to Him with wet faces, and bleared with tears for sin and the manifold troubles of this life; and Christ meets them in the door, with a fair soft napkin in His hand, and puts up His hand to

their faces, and says, " Hold your tongue, My dear bairns; ye shall never weep again." And indeed, in my judgment, it is a speech borrowed from a mother that has a bairn with a broken face, all bloody and all bleared with tears, and it comes to her (and woe's her heart to see him so), and she sits down and wipes the tears from his eyes, and lays her hand softly on the wound, and his head in her breast, and wipes away the blood, and lays her two arms about him, and there is no end of fair words. So when Christ and we shall meet in heaven, He will hush us, and wipe away all tears, and lay our head in His bosom. See how He alludes to this place (Isaiah 54. 11), "O thou afflicted, tossed with tempest, and not comforted, behold, I will lay thy foundations with sapphires," It is there, to speak so, our Lord is repenting that ever He had handled the saints as He did. (Isaiah 65: 18, 19), "Be glad and rejoice for ever in that which I create; for, behold, I create Jerusalem a rejoicing, and her people a joy. And I will rejoice in Jerusalem, and joy in My people: and the voice of weeping shall be no more heard in her, nor the voice of crying." If ever there was a happy meeting betwixt two, it must be betwixt the Bridegroom and the bride in the marriage-day. And what a meeting there is of joy betwixt such a Bridegroom and bride cannot be conceived. For Christ that day will have on all His best clothes. And such a bride as the Lamb's wife! when we shall be clothed, and not a wrong pin on us; a fair bride in silk and purple of Christ's own dressing. And what a welcome she will get! To get a drink at our first meeting and incoming to heaven, "of the well of the water of life." Oh, strong comforting water! And Christ our Lord shall present His bride to His Father; and our Father-in-law, the Father of our Husband, shall take us by the hand and lead us to the inner part of the house to the dining hall, and set us down at a table to feast our fill upon "the tree of life" - to feast upon the Trinity for evermore! Now, mock and scorn the way to heaven as ye please; ye never heard of true happiness till now. Here is a "banquet of joy" for evermore.

"He shall wipe away all tears." - Christ our Lord in this world wipes the tears from His bairns' faces; yet after that they weep new tears. He never wipes away *all* tears till now. Here shall be our last "good- night" to death - good-night to crying, and mourning, and sorrow! We shall be on the other side of the water, and over beyond

the black river of death, and shall scorn death; for Christ shall take death and hell and cast them in the prison of fire (Rev. 20: 14). The mother that lost her bairns shall get them - all the Lord's widows shall get their husbands - the old world, which was the mourning world, shall be away. And therefore, never till now shall "*all* tears" be wiped away.

The Kirk is half a widow here; her Lord is in an uncouth country; far from her home: and *ilk loon* (each low fellow) round about plucks at this feeble widow, while she is in the valley of Baca, wherein is no water. The watchmen strike her and take her veil from her; but Christ writes a love letter to her, and after she has read it she rejoiceth and wipeth her face. But when the letter grows old, and she has lost the letter, new troubles come on; she sheds new tears, and comes under new persecutions; and her Lord, for her sins, goes in behind the wall and hides Himself, and lets her mourn her fill. But in that day "He will wipe away all tears from her eyes." See then how it goes here in this life - first a fair day, then again a foul day, till at last that fair day dawns when all shadows flee away; and there shall never be a foul day after that; but aye the long, lasting, summer day for evermore. You see a man travelling to his home - here is a water, then dry land; then another water, then dry land; then a water, and at last only dry land between him and his home: then he goes home to his wife and bairns, and has no more waters. So all our tears are never dried till we come to heaven; for the saints have a liferent tack of the cross of Christ, while we are here, and aye ill weather -(Matt. 16:16)- ever the cross. See in John 16: 20 & 22, our Lord compares our troubles to the pains that come upon a woman in travailing; now a shower, and then some ease; a shower again, and then ease - aye till the last shower that she be delivered, and then no more showers: "She remembereth no more the anguish, for joy that a man is born into the world." We must be in pain ere our birth be born; but we shall be delivered of our birth.

Let us prepare; for tears will follow us to heaven; unto the very entry of the door our face shall be wet, for we go out of this life sad and groaning for this miserable life; and to thrust through the last port, and to wade through the hindermost water - it is a sore set. But be cheerful Christians, and grip to the promises. God's bairns that can now mourn for their own sins, and the sins of the land, rejoice in heaven; there are never seen greeting baims there; God has a napkin to wipe their faces. It is the laughing, rejoicing people that God destroys. But ye that laugh now (Luke 6: 25), (and are so far from tears - that ye mock the mourners of Zion), you may sigh and close the Bible, and say, "Alas! I never shed a tear for Christ: your text is not for me." It may be Christ shall that day make you weep and shed tears for evermore. This sour, laughing world will pass away - there is a day of tears coming on you; "greeting and gnashing of teeth." And when a man gnasheth his teeth, one against another, he has no mind of laughing. I would not have your mirth for a world. Be doing; we shall see who will laugh fastest yon day.

There is an ill coming on this land. Sin is not come to full harvest. Often have I told you of a fan of God's word to come among you, for the contempt of it. I have told you often of wrath - wrath from the Lord to come upon Scotland, and yet I bide by my Master's word; it is quickly coming - desolaton for Scotland, because of the quarrel of a broken covenant. Now, my dear people, my joy and crown, seek the Lord and His face; let Him be your fear. "Flee to your stronghold, ye prisoners of hope." Doves, flee to Christ's windows, and save your souls.

Verse 5. *"And He that sat upon the throne said, Behold, I make all things new. And He said unto me, Write; for these words are true and faithful."*

John heareth more of Christ - a sweet speech. Here are three things mentioned – First: a speaker; Second: a speech; Third: a direction to keep the speech.

I. A speaker. " *He that sat upon the throne.* " - Who spake the speech is not told, whether an angel or an earthly king, for they sit on thrones also. But it is He of whom it is said (Rev. 4: 2), "And behold a throne was set in heaven, and one sat on the throne." John tells not His name, but he thinks so much of Him, that he takes it for granted that there is none worthy to be a King but He, and to sit on a throne but He. The saints measure all the affections of others by their own affections. As, if one inquired of John, "Who is He that sits upon the throne?" he would have answered, " What needs you ask? Is there any in heaven or earth, in my estimation, worthy to be a King but He? and to sit on a throne but He? and to take a crown upon His head but He? "The saints set aye Christ alone - they set Him above all. Speak of kings to them; but Christ is out of play. So (Song of Solomon 3: 3), the Kirk, meeting with "the watchmen," saith, "Saw ye Him whom my soul loveth?" What knew the watchman of Him whom her soul loved? For she might have loved a loon, or a harlot, or an idol-god, or the world. But she measureth the watchman by herself. There was none in *her* mind but Christ; and therefore she needed not to tell them, as she thought. So Mary Magdalene (John 20: 15) says to the gardener (as she thought), "Sir, if ye have borne Him hence, tell me where ye have laid Him. She tells not what *Him,* taking as granted, that what so much possessed her own soul would doubtless equally occupy the thoughts of every other; and none was so much in her mind as Christ. Now, I pray you let the same mind be in you that was in John and in Mary. Let Christ be to your soul the pearl of the ring. Among all kings, Christ should be made high, and esteemed by us as He - the only He - that is worthy to "sit on a throne." So, in Song of Solomon 5:10, He is to the Kirk "the chiefest among ten thousand." Gather all the angels in heaven and earth together; Christ is too good to be their Captain. And, indeed what is all that sits on a throne? It must be infinitely more in Him. And whatever glory is in the world is far more in Him. Take all the roses in the earth, and put them all in one, that would be a dainty thing and sight. But what are all these to Christ? - No more than a nettle to the fairest rose. Fie upon the tasteless love of men, that never loveth Jesus Christ, and yet falleth in love with lusts. They love gold, riches, and honour, and put Christ to a backside. Ay, Christ gets not His own among us. We recommend Him not; neither will we match with Him.

2. A speech. *"I will make all things new"* – This is as much as all things are old. Sin hath made all things old. They are like a woman groaning in childbirth with pain and vanity, because of our sin (Romans 8: 22). All the creatures are sickened because of sin. Because of our sin, vanity came on the sun, moon, and other creatures. They sigh under this, and pray, in their kind, a *malison* (evil; curse) and a woe to man, for sin has made us all miserable. The heavens, that are the fairest part of the great web of the world, "wax old as a garment;

"the prophet saith they are like an old clout. The water saith, "Let me drown sinners - they have sinned against my Lord;" the fire saith, "Let me burn them - let me burn Sodom, for they have sinned against my Lord." All things have lost the glory that they got at their first creation. Jesus seeth all things gone wrong, and quite out of order, and man fallen from his Lord. And He did even with the world as the pilot, who, when an inattentive man at the rudder was steering the ship on a sandbank, stept in quickly and turned her incontinent, or else all would have gone to confusion. So our Lord stept in when the great ship of this world was running on a sand bed; and when the sun and the moon looked sad-like, and said they would not serve us, He renewed them by His death, made them all laugh on the elect again, and gave them all a suit of new clothes.

Drunkards, Christ gave His blessing on the wine that ye spue on the walls. Ye that dishonour your Maker with your vain apparel, ye know not what it cost Christ our Lord to buy a right to those things that ye abuse in vanity. All that set the world in their hearts, where the Lord should be, forget that Christ bought the world to be their servant, and not to be as their darling and wife that lies in their bosom. Ye that make the earth, and the broad acres of it, your soul's portion, forget that Christ bought the earth, and made it new, to be a footstool, and not a chair for our souls to sit down in. And if Christ has this art to make all things new, come to Him all ye that are old. Oh, ye that have old hearts, come. Christ may get His craft among ye, if ye would come to Him. "He makes all things new." The devil has borrowed your heart for covetousness, and crooked it with the thorny cares of this world, and holed it, and knocked the bottom out of it. Oh! if ye would put it in Christ's hand, He would put it into His furnace, and melt it again, and by His art bring it out a new heart for Himself to dwell in. Alas! Christ gets not His trade or calling among us. But why are not our old hearts mended? Because we handle them as a foolish mother doth her *dawted* bairn (indulged child); she will not let him go to the school to learn, and why? - Because she does not want him out of her sight. She will therefore never let him do well, but feeds him for the gallows. We *dow* (dare not; cannot) not give away our souls to Christ, who would fain have, and could easily mend them. But lust, or pride, or covetousness, like the foolish mother, keeps them out of Christ's company; so that we will not let that dear craftsman, who made the earth under our feet and the mountains new, make our old hearts new. Our souls are all hanging in tatters, worn and old with sin, and yet we dow not put them in Christ's hand, that He might make them whole and cleanse them. Fie upon thee, that thy garden, cursed in Adam's day to bring forth nettles and thorns, is blessed again to bring forth fruit in Christ, and thy soul gets not so much of Him as thy yard; it is made new, but thy soul remains old. Oh! Bring it to Jesus; He will create in you a clean heart, and renew a right spirit within you. Indeed, Christ may get His craft among ye, if you would go to Him; for it is His trade to "make all things new."

3. A direction to keep the speech. "*And He said unto me, Write; for these words are true and faithful.*" He bids John write these things about the state of the glorified, and calls them faithful and true. He would not entrust His word to man's memory and conscience - He would have it written. Blasphemous Papists, laugh not at this, nor call the Pope's breast the Bible; here is a warrant for written Scripture. Indeed, it tells us that man's falsehood wore his conscience. Had his conscience been a faithful register, there should have been no need of a written Bible. But now the Lord has *lippened* (trusted) more to dead paper than to a living man's soul. Our conscience, now under sin, had not been a good Bible, because man is ready to run away from his conscience, and because what is written on our conscience (as, that there is a God - a judgment - a heaven - a hell), Satan and sin come in as two false witnesses and blot it out, and write that in the fool's heart that says, "There is no God." And there are many holes in our souls; the word of God comes in and runs out again at back spouts, except Jesus makes our souls water fast, so that "the word of God may dwell in us plentifully" (Colossians 3: 16). Are not our hearts compared to a field, wherein the preacher sows the seed, and the black spirits of hell come and gather up Christ's wheat? Oh! but there are many running-out souls; and much need we have of a written Bible. Therefore make much of the written word, and pray God to copy His Bible into your conscience, and write a new book of His doctrine in your hearts, and put it in the conscience as He directs (Jeremiah 31.)

Verse 6. *"And He said unto me, It is done. I am Alpha and Omega, the beginning and the end. I will give unto him that is athirst of the fountain of the water of life freely."*

Here, also, are three things – First: a prophecy; Second: a description; Third: a promise of water.

I. A prophecy. Christ says to John, *"It is done."* - That is exponed in Revelation 16 & 17. The world is ended. So speaks Christ of the world. The glory of it passeth away in the twinkling of an eye, and Christ crieth to those that have the world in both their arms. "It is done"; it is a past thing, there is no more of it. It is but a word to our Lord. He said, "Let all things be," and they were; He will say, "Let all things depart," and they will be at an end. We are beginning with the world as if it would be evermore ours; and our Lord says, in a moment "Let it be plucked from them," and it is done. It is not for nothing that the taking down of this inn of heaven and earth is touched in so few words - "It is done." For it is an easy thing for the Almighty to take in His own hand the staves that hold up this fat tent, and when He pulleth it, He *garreth* (compels; causes) it come down with a tilt. So (Revelation 7: 1), four angels are brought in, "holding the four winds of the earth," as if they had the world in their hands, and as if they had it ready to fold up as a sheet. And oh! what a fighting and business do men make to get a *clout* (a piece of linen rag) of this sheet! - he staring out his eyes - and he setting out his neck, for a piece of this holly (tattered) clout and sheet, and for a *gloib* (piece of ground) of the earth. But (see Revelation 6:14) "The heavens shall depart away like a scroll" (parchment that is rolled together, and the fair stories thereof are like figs); with the shake of the Almighty's arm shall they fall together to the ground. And, what is more, with a touch of the Almighty's hand, or a putt of His little finger, or a blast of His mouth, saying, "It is done," *the cupples* (two rafters joined at the top) of the walls of the house shall come down. Now, I cannot but speak of fools that have their heads full of windmills, and cry it is beginning, "To-morrow shall be as this day, and much more abundant" (Isaiah 56:12), and there is no end of buying and selling. I came not here to bid anybody be unthrifty; but be not like bairns building sandy *bourocks* (places of shelter) at a burn-side, when presently a speat of water comes and spills all their sport, or a shower chases them in from their play. Men are ever building castles in the air. In very deed, we are like bairns holding the water at a riverside with their hands. They think (out of their right mind) they hold the water, while in the meantime it runs through their fingers. And what says God of honour, riches, pleasure, lands, fair houses, and sums of money? Even that in a word, "all is done." Ask of them that had the world and broad acres once at will what is to the fore? And what is to the fore of so many thousands? What has the world of them but their name? And what if their name be lost too? For what is their name? Ten or eleven letters of the A B C; and for their bodies - howbeit, when they were living, kingdoms would not content them - the clay into which their bodies are dissolved would not now fill a glove. I think that a true and a strange spoken word (Isaiah 11: 22), "God sitteth upon the circle of the earth, and the inhabitants thereof are as grasshoppers." We even creep like grasshoppers up and down the globe of this earth, and cry to men of the vanities of all things, while death comes, like a common thief, without any din or feet, and plucks them away, and there is no more of them; then they say, "It is done." All men must confess it is true that I say; but I think to be dead ere they believe it, and act accordingly, or be brought to hate the world. I think the world is the devil's great herry-water-net, (great trawling net) that has taken thousands and slain them. Ye say ye are sure of it. Then I say ye are a *dieted* (well fed) horse for heaven.

2. The second thing that is in the verse is a description of Christ: "*I am Alpha and Omega, the beginning and the end.*" Our Lord here being to make an offer of the water of life, He first showeth what He is - even the first and the last letter of the alphabet - the Ancient of Days - the Eternal Son of the Eternal God. This teaches us that we may *crack* (talk freely) more of our old holding, and old charter, than all the world can do. For why? When began Christ to bear a good will to a sinner? Even when He began to be God; and He was God from all eternity. Suppose the sun in the firmament was eternal, the light of it behoved to be eternal; for the light of the sun is as old as the sun. Now love is a beam of life and heat that comes from Christ, the Sun of Righteousness; therefore ever living Christ - ever living love. For love comes not on Christ the day, which was not in

Him yesterday. Man's love and a king's love are hunted for very much; and yet they die, and their love dies with them, and often their love dies before themselves. But who seeks Christ's love, that "changes not?" Yea, this a matter of admiration and wonder, that Christ should have thought on us worms of the clay ere ever we were, and that our salvation is as old as evermore - as old as Christ, and Christ is as old as God!

Indeed, if God should begin at any point of time to love sinners, His love would have had a beginning; and if His love had a beginning, Christ Himself would have had a beginning, because love with Him is one with His essence and nature. But it may be said, can the love of God be older than the death of Christ? *Answer.* Christ's death doth not properly make God a hater or a lover of man; for then both His will should be changeable and His love have a beginning. How then? Christ's death doth only let that God *kythe* (permit God to show) the fruits of His eternal love out upon us, but after such a way as He thought convenient for His justice; and therefore *we* are said in Scripture "to be reconciled unto God," and not God to be reconciled unto us. His love is everlasting; because by order of nature it was before the seed, before we had done either good or evil; so that sin could not change God's mind. But only by the order of justice, sin stood in the way to hinder us of life everlasting, which is a fruit of His love. Yea, more, God with that same love in Christ, loveth the elect before and after conversion; and therefore, in feeling any of God's love to us, we have to rejoice in Christ. It is old acquaintance between Him and us. And therefore, as it is folly in man (as Solomon saith) to cast off his old friend, and his father's friend, so let us think it madness to cast off such an old friend as Christ. And under temptations and desertions, let our faith hold fast by this - Alpha and Omega changeth not; the change is in us.

3. The third thing in the words is a promise of the water of life to the thirsty – "*I will give unto him that is athirst of the fountain of the water of life freely.*" (Isaiah 55: 1, and John 4:14). Christ at the market- cross cries the well free. Here learn,

First: The thirsty and hungry souls are meetest for the water of life. What! (ye will say) and are not all thirsty? Yes; all want the life of God, and the sap of grace, and are burnt and withered at the root;

but all know not their own want. Here is indeed a special comfort
for the weak ones who say, "Oh! I know Christ doth good to believers,
to repenters, and to such as love Him; but I dow not, cannot, win to
faith and repentance, hope and patience; I have too short an arm to
reach so high." Then, say I, have ye a desire - a hunger - for faith,
and repentance, and love? Now, upon your conscience, speak the
truth. I trow ye cannot deny it. Then your Lord bids you come - the
well is open to you; for hunger and thirst being next to motion, and
the two properties that begin first with life, so every one that is newborn is lively, and hath a stomach for meat and drink. "Oh but," say
ye, "I am many times, in my soul, at death's door. I have neither
faith nor feeling. I am even at this -'God loves me not,' and the well
is not ordained for me at these times." Would ye fain be at the well?
In my mind ye cannot win away. In the children of God, when at the
lowest ebb - even when faith, comfort, joy, love, and disposition to
pray are away, is there not a longing for a presence? I speak to the
conscience of God's child; lie not. David (Psalm 6:), when he thought
God spake to him in wrath, was at, "How long, Lord?" - a cutting
word. I think I looked like a hungry beast looking over the dyke; he
would fain have a mouthful. He was going about to seek a *slap* (an
opening) to break over the dyke of his doubtings. And so it is with
God's bairns, under their thirst for the water of the well of life. See
Song of Solomon 3: when the Kirk can get no speiring of Christ,
and has no smell of Him, and cannot find the print of His foot, yet
she is at this, "Saw ye Him whom my soul loveth?" And (chap. 5:
8), "I charge you, O daughters of Jerusalem, if ye find my Beloved,
that ye tell Him, that I am sick of love." Then let me now tell you
weak ones who are Christ's companions, and who it is shall drink
with Him, and get their hearts and heads full of the water of life -
even the tender Christians that are aye seeking. The bairn in Christ's
house that is most cumbersome, and makes most din for his meat, is
the best bairn that Christ has. The bairn that is greetingt ilk hour of
the day for a piece and a drink - we say of such a silly thing, "He
would fain love." Aye, the cumbersomer that Christ's bairns be, they
are welcomer. Na, He loveth the bairns best that have no shame, and
are aye crying, "Alas! black hunger, dear Lord Jesus; I am burnt
with thirst; oh for an open cold fountain!" Oh, it is a sweet thing aye

to be whinging, and crying, and seeking about Christ's pantry doors, and to hold aye an eye upon Christ when He goes into the house of wine, into His Father's fair lucky wine-cellar, where there are many wines; and push in at Christ's back! But, in a word, have ye a good stomach? - much hunger and thirst? Well, ye shall get much satisfaction of grace in Christ. Is there not a time when ye cannot get a presence, and ye have no pith to put up the door and bout in, but ye put it half up and blink in? Love ye to pray, or desire ye but a desire of prayer? Hold on then; ye are right. The true desire is absolute, and not conditional. Not like the sluggard that would have a crop, upon condition he might have a feather bed to lie on for fear of cold. Even so some would have heaven, upon condition that they might keep their lusts, and take their lusts with them.

Now, who are they that are debarred from Christ's well? *Answer.* Those who have gotten an ill drink from the devil, full of lusts, pride, and covetousness - full of love of the world. Such are they that have no stomach for Christ. Alas and woes me! Christ standeth at the well's side, and crieth, "The back of My hand to you." The Lord Jesus gives such a vomit-drink, that they may grow wholesome and hungry again for Christ; for till then they are never meet for Him.

But secondly, hunger is aye seeking through the house; for the belly can hardly play the hypocrite The natural man is in darkness - he is in a sleep - it is night with him. He is like a cumbersome bairn greeting in the night for a drink, and crying, "Who will shew me any good?" (Psalm 4: 6). And Satan is ready at his elbow with his dishful of the dirty, miry waters of lust to the world; and he drinks till he sweats and *tines* (loses) breath; and tines all sight and desire of Christ, "the Fountain of the Water of Life." It is true this fountain is said to proceed "out of the throne of God and of the Lamb" (Rev. 22: 1). But it is all one; for the streams of the water of life proceed from the fountain, Christ. How, then, is the water Christ? *Answer.* It is *Christ-man,* dying, and sending out His heart's blood for quenching the thirst of such poor sinners as find the fire of hell at the stomach of their souls, burning them up with the fire of the wrath of God for sin. This is the well: this is why He is called "a fountain of the water of life." A man, burnt with thirst, nothing can quench him; no, not a world of gold is so good as a drink of pure, cold, clean, fountain water. In a word, a soul wakened under sin findeth nothing in the world satisfactory to the soul's appetite but in Christ. Tell me; art thou a thirsty sinner after Christ? Then thy soul is dead sick while ye get Him. Is a man faint, and fatigued, and wayworn? Lay him down on a soft bed, dry the sweat off him, and give him a cold refreshing drink. In like manner, ye cannot speak such a word to a soul bursting under sin, as to lay it upon a crucified Christ. Oh, that is a soft bed! His sinful soul being stretched upon the open wounds and warm-flowing blood of Christ. Oh, that is a soft bed! Oh, but a part of Christ's blood is a refreshing, cooling drink to him! A slave of hell to know that he is made a free heir of heaven - oh, that is sweet! Hence it is that those who are wakened with the furies of hell, howbeit they know not yet what Christ is to them, yet this world cannot calm their conscience, because for men that are soul-sick and sin-sick there is no physic but one only, a "drink of the well of life." And because they ken not the gate to this well of life, they, in despair, leap out of this life into the fire of hell, through the madness of an awakened conscience. A thirsty soul finds two things in Christ, never to be found in all the world or in anything else.

First: Christ takes off the hardness of sin. None has power to do this but He. All the pardons of sin are in Christ's keeping, and of Christ's making. It is His office to forgive sin. Second: They find in Him an influence and abundance of happiness, so as what they sought before in the creature, they find nowhere else but in Him. Then speak to them of gold – it is nothing to Christ. Speak of lands and lordships - a Saviour, and such a Saviour, is, and has another name to a sinner that is awakened. Third: The text calls Him *"the water of life."* We see here there is some water that is rotten and ill tasted. Will a thirsty man drink of it? He shall not be the better. But the wholesomest water is the running spring; so all that sinners can get beside Christ is standing water. Let them drink in gold, and kingdoms, and lands; these will never be satisfying to a sick soul as He will be. And they who have drunk in these, at death would be content to spue them out again; they lie so heavy upon their stomach. But Christ is the cooling, wholesome spring - "the well of water springing up to eternal life." Now, make our use of this. Seeing Christ is such a living well of water, how comes it that under the gospel there are so many dry and withered souls? I answer for God's part, indeed, God has not put an iron lock upon the well of life; but Christ, by His word and sacraments, opens the well in the midst of us, and for seventy years and more in this kingdom the well has been open - Christ and His messengers have been crying to dry souls. But now, for aught we see, He will close the well again. He has been setting out the means of life, and opening the booth-doors to give us freely, even to such as would take it; but He gets no sale. Therefore He must put up His wares and go away, for men are not thirsty for His waters. But one thirsts for court and honour, another for lust and money, and a third for sinful pleasures. There be few stomachs gaping for Christ. They have not a vessel to cast down into the well and take up water. This is a fruitless generation. Oh, we loathe Christ, and Christ loathes us. We need speak no more of the call of the word. All the land - court, king, noblemen, and kirkmen - have spued the waters, by despising grace and contemning the gospel; and in very deed, when we cast in clay and mud in Christ's well, and mix His worship with the poison of the whore's well of Rome, what do we else but provoke the Lord to close the well?

"I will give it freely." So are all Christ's mercies given of grace. His mercy is for nothing, and of free grace. I grant the well is dear to Christ. God's justice digged it out of His side, and heart, and hands, and feet. The man, Christ, got not this water for nothing; yet He gives it to us for nothing, because He minds not to make a gain of us. We live upon Christ's winning. For know ye that Christ, who redeemed many, did so, by the rule of justice, since "He gave Himself," and has bought all "with His own blood;" so that in this sense Christ was bought to us with blood, else we could not get Him, for He was both the price and the wares. So that, as far as we can see, it was decreed by the Lord, by order of justice, that Christ could not have lived and given to us the waters of life. It was dear water to Him; for in the garden God deserted Him, and blood came out; on the cross God bruised Him, and blood came out; and *that* is the well we have here. We think we would have something to give to Christ for the water of life – some of our own righteousness - some of our own worthiness; but this is *plastered humiliy watered* (plated and gilded) copper. And in doing so we refuse grace and make grace to be no

more grace; for if it be given for any worth in us, then it is no more grace. Let men here see, then, that the kingdom of grace is a good, cheap world, where the best things are gotten for nothing. And therefore, I think in this dear world, where all things go for money, whose court costs are expensive, lands are dear, gold is not gotten for nought, and law is dearer than ever it was. Yea, paper and ink are dearer than jewels and gold rings were long syne. Nothing now is bought for nought. Yet Christ for all that will not change His word. All things with Him are given *gratis,* and ye are welcome when all is done. Here we get no garments for nought, no physic for nought; but Christ gives "white raiment," "eye salve," and all for nought. Sinners say, "Lord, what take Ye for the water of life?" He answers, "Even nothing, and yet welcome." Christ plays not the merchant with His wares: He makes no gain, but cries, "The well is free". No, says the Pope - not a drop of it, till ye tell down money. That bloody Beast would sell the water of Rome for gold. As meikle money - as meikle grace and forgiveness. Want ye money? (He swears) Ye shall not come here. Nothing in Rome without money. Fie, fie, the stink of the devil's world. Nay, but Christ is for nothing. Nay, justice giveth money, and officers give money; it is a dear world. But Christ and His word care no more for money than before. (Than if there were no Pope and world.

Verse 7. "*He that overcometh shall inherit all things; and I will be his God and he shall be My son.*"

I. Always in this book John urgeth "fighting" and "overcoming" for heaven. We wonder much that God will not have poor men go to heaven but by fighting, seeing He might have sent us to heaven by a second heaven. But this is but a thought of men that would make a new back-gate of their own to heaven. God advised well when He made His causeway to it, and ordained all His saints, yea, His own Son, to go that way. But it is easier for us to complain on God's decree than to obey, and to dispute than believe. Men have too thin skins. For health, they will cut a vein, or let a leg or an arm be cut off for fear of a fester; and yet for "life everlasting" they are so, that they dare not venture a moment's pain.

2. There are excellent promises made to the overcomers - to him that taketh heaven with stroke of sword and blood. For heaven is a

besieged city or castle. There are many foes to fight against. Armies of sin with all their armour, and the deceiving and malicious world. The world has Eve's apple in one hand, and fire and sword in the other; and the devil is the captain of the army. Now, here is a prize set, and an offer made to him that overcometh - to him that will mount up by faith and hope, and leap up into Christ's chariot, and betide him life, betide him death, will go through. But they are cowards that take a back-side, and let the devil coup them in a gutter. But yet to lead men on, here is a promise, "He shall inherit all things." Ye see that the Christians' Captain is a man of a fair rent; "for all things are yours, whether Paul, or Apollos, or Cephas, or the world, or life, or death, or things present, or things to come, all are yours." (I Cor. 3: 21, 22). And to let us see He bides by the thing He has said, He says again, "All things are yours." Ye see in this world one has a kingdom, as Asa, but wants health, and is sick of his feet; he has not all things. Another, as Samson, had strength of body above any living, yet he had many troubles and wanted his eyes; he had not all things. Oh, the business Adam's sons are at for inheritances! Here a *mailen* (farm) - there a lairdship - there a new lordship. That they call their all things. I think this is a greedy style, and proud-like lordship or lairdship. Yet, greedy Adam's sons have more greediness here than wit. They run all upon their lordships, that they call the lordship of many things. "Martha, Martha, thou art troubled." (Luke 10: 41) Worldlings, ye are aye careful and troubled about this, to be called "My lord" of many things. But we shall see if the text be true.

"I am Alpha and Omega." Ye will notice that Paul puts in "death" into the rent-roll. I think death an ill mailen; better want it out of the charter. Nay, but death is also a part of the lordship this way (because it is "My lord of all things"), and a coach to glory - Christ Himself being the coachman and driving the horse. Death is the servant. As the wind serveth to bring the seaman home, so death serveth him that hath the new lordship. Death is Christ's ferryboat to carry the Christian home, for in Christ he sets his foot on death's neck. It is a bridge over the river of hell that he walketh on to heaven; and it is his. The Christian is advanced in Christ's court, and gets the new style to be "My lord of all things," the prince, the duke of all things.

Yet I shall get you a lordship far inferior, but much sought for - the lordship of vanity or nothing. "Wilt thou set thine eyes upon that which is not?" He that is rich has nought; "for riches certainly make themselves wings - they flyaway as an eagle towards heaven " (Prov. 23: 5).

2. Again, if the Christian *"inherits all things, "* the whole world is his, and so he wanteth nothing. (Psalm 89: 25), "I will set his hand also in the sea, and his right hand in the rivers. "Here see how broad Christ's two arms are. His one hand upon all the sea, and His other hand upon the rivers. And that promise is made to Christ as principal cautioner of the covenant; for it is said (verse 26), "He shall cry unto Me, Thou art My Father, My God, and the rock of My salvation." Verse 27, "Also, I will make Him My first-born, higher than the kings of the earth," which is exponed of Christ (Heb. 1: 6). Again, in Rev. 10: 2, He has "His right foot on the sea and His left foot on the earth." Put these two together, and see how wide His arms and legs, or feet, are. They go over the whole world as His inheritance, which He won to Himself, and His heirs after Him, with His blood. Now, Christ got land not to Himself. What! needed He land? and to give His blood for clay? But He won it to us, and took infeftment in the earth, in the name of His friends; so that in Him they inherit "all things."

3. But here one may say, "How is it, then, that the saints are hungry and poor? *Answer.* It is true; they are not now possessors of all things. But minors' wants - ye see their interest is in and over all things, yet their tutor lets them go with a toom (empty) purse. He knows the heir is a young one, and cannot keep gold, and therefore he gives him food and raiment for his present necessity, but keeps the lordship till he be able to guide it. Even so Christ is made of God, our Tutor and Purse-Master. It is all one whether our wealth be in our chest-nook or if it be in Christ's purse, to keep till we need it, providing we want not.

Another question and doubt is, "Seeing they are under so many troubles in this life, and have no ease, the saints have not 'all things'? I answer, Yes; I must defend it, and say, if they have the *inheritance* they have all things, because the sweet and the comforts of trouble is theirs.

A third question or objection is, the saints have not heaven and glory, at least, in this life, and therefore they have not all things. I answer, 1. The promise is not fulfilled in this life. Yet, when a man has shorn a stock or two of corn, we say he "has got harvest and new corn!" So the believer gets joy, hope, faith, assurance of heaven, and the first fruits of the Spirit. These are a foretaste of the full harvest and new corn. 2. Having God and Christ, the saints have all things. For ye see the great ship draggeth the cockboat after her, so the great Christ bringeth all things after Him at His back. So I say, having Christ, believers, ye have all things - ye have "the Father and the Spirit, the word, life, and death." Amen.

THE FORLORN SON
- THE FATHER'S EXPRESSED WELCOME

But the father said to his servants, Bring forth the best robe, and put it on him; and put a ring on his hand, and shoes on his feet: and bring hither the fatted calf, and kill it; and let us eat, and be merry. Luke 15: 22-23.

Who has such opportunity, beloved in our Lord, of our Lord's kindness to a soul running to a free Saviour as those who have once been rebels and are come home again to their Lord and Father. None can sing mercies' song so well as they who can do it out of sense and experience. None can do this so well as one who can say, "Once I was blind, but now I see. I was dead once, but now I live. Once I was a child of Satan and an heir of hell, but now I am made an adopted son of God, and an heir of heaven." Who can speak more to our Lord's commendation out of experience, nor a home-coming sinner thus made welcome to his Lord and Father again? You heard in the first part of this parable how our Lord was pleased with this forlorn son, and what welcome the father gave him, or ever he spake one word of apology for himself, or ever he made any prayer at all, his father fell upon his neck and kissed him, for he waited not upon our God to move Him to be merciful unto us. He will not wait till He gets a hire for His mercy. He waits not till we make some way on our part for any good He is to do to us. He may not look for anything from us that will down-weigh the weights of His free love. O! so weighty as that is, there is much telling there. Nothing in us to prevent the same. But or ever this poor forlorn son speak a word he falls upon his neck and kisses him. And then when he makes his prayer to his Lord, leaving the half of that he resolved to say unspoken, God welcomes it. The Son of God, the same Lord who is here called Father, He passed by all the slips of his prayer, and commands that he be received by the servants of the house as a son and not as a servant. And truly they will be very feckless and confused prayers that come from any spunk of faith that our Lord will not accept and make welcome. Yea, in Hosea 14: 2, he teaches His Kirk what to say to Him when they come: "Take with you words, and turn to the

Lord: say unto Him, Take away all iniquity, and receive us graciously: so will we render the calves of our lips." He will take half-prayers, or He wants all, even prayers where words are missed, and the meaning they intended to be at. Ay, He will take sighing and sobbing for prayer, the lifting up of the hands, or of the eyes, so content is He with what His Spirit says, however it be said, as it is in Romans 8: 26, He knows the meaning of the Spirit. He seeks no more for a prayer at some times but a believing sigh that is a work of His Spirit.

And when we know not what we are doing, He knows well enough the meaning of His own Spirit, and can put a perfect commentary upon that, albeit we know not what it will do, that no man should think the Lord will not hear their prayers, because they have not good oratory to speak to the Lord in prayer, because they cannot speak as a print book, and set all the words in order, and so leave off to pray to the Lord. No, the Lord He hears the very breathing of His Kirk, (Lamentations 3: 56). Ay, when His children cannot speak, and they have no words to say to Him for what they would be at, they nay be confident to be heard, for many a dumb beggar has gotten almost at His door. They who cannot set their words in good method and order in prayer, if their heart look honestly toward the Lord, then He accepts of the sighs and good meaning of such, and takes that for prayer, and will answer it. So that all who come to Christ as they are bidden, and come in truth and sincerity, may be comforted in this, that their prayers shall not be cast away of Him.

Now, we have the expressed welcome of the Lord towards his forlorn son, and the direction and charge he gives unto his servants for getting ornaments for his body, and entertainment for cheering himself and all the house. For the ornaments that he gives direction to get, it stands in three particulars: First: That they get the best robe and put it upon the homecoming sinner. Like enough he was ragged, or he came home, as all are ill clad when they come first to Christ. Second: He commands them to get a ring upon his finger, that is an ornament of honour; and then, Third: To put shoes upon his feet. And then for expression of the joy of the Lord's mind, and the joy of the whole soul, and that all that hear what the Lord has done may be allured thereby, the fat calf is slain that all may rejoice at the home-coming of a lost sinner.

O! the rejoicing that our Lord and all the angels make for the homecoming of a lost sinner. There is more joy in heaven for the recovery of one lost sinner than there is for ninety and nine righteous persons. The Lord He knows not how to express His joyfulness and His kindness to a sinner who acknowledges what he has been doing, and repents of his misdeeds! O! repentance, it is an unknown work. Repentance is not known to be so acceptable a sacrifice to the Lord, as indeed it is. A homecoming soul that can get a bleeding heart for sin, that can thrust out an honest tear before the Lord for sin committed against Him, it knows not that God has a bottle to catch that in. They know not that God writes down all their sighs and their sobs, their tears and their sad looks. And because this is not known by the most part, therefore repentance is a slighted and neglected work. The world loves nothing worse than sorrow for sin. They think it a sad and melancholious thing; but there is no joy hereaway comparable to that joy which proceeds from an honest tear shed for sin, and for offending such a majesty as we have to do with.

Now, the first ornament that our Lord commands to be put upon this prodigal is *"The best robe."* He commands to put a robe upon him, and the best of the robes.

There is no necessity that we should strike largely upon every particular in a parable, if the main scope of the parable be looked unto. And yet there is little in this parable that looks not clearly to point out the state of a sinner in the state of sin, and to show the Lord's welcoming when they return to Him, and to let us see what ornaments He puts upon them when they come to Him.

First: Ye see he is to be clothed with a *robe,* and with *the best robe.* While a sinner is in the state of sin he is a ragged creature, and so has need of a robe, if ye will consider him two ways. If ye will consider him as he is, a man in nature, or if ye will consider him as he is, a civil righteous man; for man of himself, as he is a natural man, has no righteousness at all, or if he have any righteousness if he will say, it is as the phrase is, "A clout with many a hole in it," like that garment spoken of Job 8: 14; it is like the spider's web, that garment of man's righteousness - it holds no wind away. All our righteousness is like a menstruous clout (Isaiah. 64: 6). And you will find that all the garments that the natural man, while he is in the state of nature, they are so indeed. For while he has them he is not honest; nor marriage like to be married upon such a bridegroom as Christ. So long as we have no other garment but only our own natural righteousness, it is nothing else but sin, defiled further with sin. Isaiah 59: 6: "Their webs shall not become garments, neither shall they cover themselves with their works; their works are works of iniquity, and the act of violence is in their hands." The works of the natural man are compared there to webs, but their webs will not cover them, for the best things they do there are violence in them and unrighteousness. All those who would be married upon Christ, and would be gifted new with Him for evermore, they must have another covering upon them than their own works, or their civil righteousness. There are two things in all natural garments that make them faulty.

First: That no natural garment we can have is able to hold away the cold from us. All those who stand to be Pharisees in the act of justification by the works of the law, or by their own righteousness, they shall be forced at last to say that it will not be able to hold out the rain of the Lord's indignation. And therefore David says, "And enter not into judgment with Thy servant, for in Thy sight no flesh living shall be justified" (Psalm 143: 2). "If Thou, Lord, should mark iniquities, O Lord, who shall stand." (Psalm 130: 3). All these and many more places. They are shamed both with the lining and the outer half of their garments, which are only covered with nature and civil honesty, and with a seeming righteousness that the natural man counts so much of.

Another fault in a natural garment is that it is not honest before the Lord. It will be long ere ever God give that commendation to a natural and outward righteous man, that He gives to His spouse in the Song of Solomon: "Thou art all fair, my beloved, thou art all fair: there is no spot in thee." Long or thou smell in his nostrils of myrrh, aloes, cassia, and cinnamon. The natural and civil righteous man has no smell of heaven, or of glory. But Isaiah 64: 6, says, "They smell like a menstruous woman." All their "righteousnesses" - in the plural number - are like filthy rags that will never make a creature beautiful in the sight of God, and therefore there must be such an exchange as that which is spoken of in II Corinthians 5: 21; "He must be made sin for us who knew no sin; that we may be made the righteousness of God in Him." These two must be done ere ever we can be clean in the sight of God. Christ must be clothed with our sins, and we, again, must be clothed with His righteousness, and that is the fairest and the closest garment that any can be.

Now this garment is called "the best garment;" and it is the king's best garment, for it is the righteousness of our Lord. There may be good garments and better garments, but this is the best of all garments. Ay, this garment of Christ's righteousness is better in respect of the event, and for us, than if Adam had stood in the state he was in, and so we to have been clothed with Adam's righteousness. This is the best robe of all - the righteousness of God made ours. In Phil. 3: 8-9; the apostle says, "and do count them but dung that I may win Christ; and be found in him, not having mine own righteousness, which is of the law, but that which is through the faith of Christ, the righteousness which is of God by faith," clothed with that righteousness, that is the righteousness of Him who is both God and man. And look what wisdom of God is to be found here! And what goodness and loving-kindness! And such a supernatural providence that whereas the devil, that old serpent, had a mind by Adam's fall to bring Adam and all his posterity in the compass of eternal damnation; yet the Lord has turned about the wheel, so that so many as belong to Him in His election shall get better than they lost in Adam, a more sure and permanent and glorious estate.

This reproves those who would have the death of our Lord Jesus for sinners to come by hazard; who say that the Lord at first intended not the incarnation of Christ and His death and sufferings of itself, but at the first He principally intended Adam's obedience, creating him in the state of innocence; and that he was able to stand, but that Adam fell, and then there was a necessity of a Saviour; that He intended not principally, but it came upon our Lord by hazard. This is a wrong unto our Lord, who, from the beginning, intended the glory of His mercy and free grace, and also the glory of His justice. No; the Lord was not deprived of His first intention, as they say, and so behoved to take Him to a second thought. No; for from the beginning the Lord, intended the glory of His mercy to be manifested towards some, and to manifest the glory of His justice upon others, to the glory of His name. And we owe Him hearty thanks for this, that we should be made welcome to get the borrowed righteousness of Jesus; and if we get that, we shall be marriage-like, and our Lord will marry us. Alas! what will the outward living of many do to them without this? No; such are in the way to be lost for ever, and to be naked, so that the cold shall seize upon them, and Christ will not marry them to Him because they live and die and never see themselves to be sinners, and so cannot inherit the kingdom of God. Our Saviour says, "Unless a man be born again he cannot enter into the kingdom of heaven." The civil natural man knows not what that is to be born again, and so lives and dies without seeing himself to stand in need of Christ. He contents himself with the outward *calsay* (causeway; street) godliness, and thinks that enough to take him to heaven. But certainly if thy natural pride be not subdued, and thy worldly mindedness, thou cannot come there. If thou only seek to be approven in the eyes of the present world, that will fail you, for it is not the best robe; it is not the main thing the Lord gives His elect ones to live a civil life. But those who are clothed with the robe of Christ's righteousness it shall not fail them, but cover them from the cold.

The second ornament his father appoints for him it is a *ring upon his finger*. This is a simple ornament. We may learn from this that the lower a sinner set himself, the Lord will set him up higher. Albeit he set himself very low, the Lord will not do so also. The forlorn son would not believe when he sought a place among the servants that his father would have advanced him to be a son; he thought it much if he gat that. But now his father makes him a son, and will have him no lower, and he is adorned with the best robe, and gets a ring put upon his finger. Thus we may see, let a humbled sinner set himself very low, God will not do so to him. Also Ephesians 3: 8: "Unto me, who am less than the least of all saints is this grace given, that I should preach among the Gentiles the unsearchable riches of Christ." Paul there is little in his own conceit, but God counts not so of him also. And when Ananias makes a question, Acts 9: 13, if he shall go to Paul shortly after his conversion the Lord says, "Go" to him, "for he is a chosen vessel to carry My name through the world." The Lord gives unto the humbled sinner a high place and seat in heaven. The believer is never a whit the worse esteemed in God's books that he counts little of himself. That thou countest thyself very base and low, shall not blot thy name out of the Lamb's book of life. High shalt thou be in the Lord's books if thou humble thyself very low. Better that the Lord stoop down and take thee out of the dust than that thou shalt build thy nest among the stars with Edom, and the Lord to pull you down out of thy nest.

This speaks against many of the dear children of God that put themselves far beneath themselves, and will not let it appear that God has thoughts of peace towards them while indeed He has great and large thoughts towards them for their good. But if believers knew what thoughts God has of them, and what a royal and stately throne He has prepared for them, they would then be too glad, and would set their sails over high, and would not be so much taken up with the sense of the Lord's loving-kindness. But He will let His children mourn and walk humbly under the sense of their own unworthiness, that they may be the better fitted to make a high preaching of the Lord's goodness and free mercy, who *louts* (bends down) Himself to take up those who are so low, and respects them who are little in their own eyes and the eyes of the world about them.

The third ornament is "*shoes upon his feet.*" Albeit, it is true, we need not, neither will we, stand upon every particular, yet there is good ground for this in Scripture, that a home-coming sinner is ordained for a journey after he is come home. In Song of Solomon 7: 1, shoes are spoken of: "How beautiful are thy feet with shoes, O prince's daughter." And in Ephesians 6:15, among the rest of the pieces of the spiritual armour, we are commanded to have our "feet shod with the preparation of the gospel of peace." Why would the Lord speak this to His Kirk and children, but to let sinners know when they are come to Him, they may not be barefooted. For there are thorns and sharp rocks in the way to heaven, and therefore we have now to take heed to that exhortation set down in Hebrews 12: 13: "Make straight paths for your feet, lest that which is lame be turned out of the way." What a sweet word is that which we have in Psalm 119: 104: "I have refrained my feet from every evil way, that

I may keep Thy word." The righteous sinner must take heed where he sets his feet, and not set down his feet in every place, nor be barefooted, for there are more snares and rough passages on the way to heaven than ye believe there be. How many are there who go to heaven and sink not in some myres by the way? We have heard of none of these. It is well said that the way to heaven is like a mossy way; some wet their feet as they go through it, and yet win through at last.

But some, going on unawares, drown in a myre by the way, and never win through. The Lord's children in the way towards heaven must not be barefooted, but have shoes upon their feet, for there are many thorns in the way, as the examples of the servants of God that have gone before us declare. David's adultery and murder was a thorn strake up in his foot, and made him to halt all his days. Noah's drunkenness, and the Lord's chief disciple Peter, who in denying his Lord and Master, gets a thorn in his foot, tell us that we had great need to take heed to our feet, and to walk in Christ's way that He has gone before us, to have our feet shod against those rough ways. And how many are there in the world who live and die in adultery and harlotry, living a profane and godless life, not making conscience of swearing, drinking, breaking the Lord's day, and so lose the right gate to heaven, only because they are not shod with the shoes of the gospel of peace, and see not the right way where they should walk?

There is yet a particular to be marked which is very worthy of our observation, and it is also a part of the scope and drift of the parable, and it is this: That our Lord makes more of the forlorn son coming home again to Him than he does of the other son who had stayed at home, not departing from the house. For ye see there are no ornaments put upon the eldest son, nor any melody for his biding in the house. Where we may learn this, that repentance and rising by the grace of God out of the state of sin, is better than all the outwardly moral life and Pharisaical righteousness in the world.

And in some respects this repentance and rising by grace out of the state of sin, having fallen, is better than no sinning at all.

There are great questions about this, whether it had been better for man not to sin, or to sin and get mercy for sin. It is true, I grant, there is danger in the one which is not in the other, and in reference and respect towards us, it were better not to sin than to sin. It were better not to be sick, and so not to need the physician, than to be sick and need his cures. But if we will look unto Christ's feasts and offers that He makes unto us, having sinned, and to the Lord's comforts and refreshments He has prepared for His own, we may say that it is best. And in respect of the Lord and what He gave for repentance, He gave a dear price for repentance, a greater price than was given for Adam's not sinning; for if he had continued there needed no repentance, and it was free; but the other cost a very dear price (Acts 5:31). Christ purchased repentance. He died and rose again to purchase repentance; and therefore it must be of more worth than Adam's not sinning, seeing it cost our Lord such a price. Ye will grant that a jewel that has cost ten hundred thousand pounds must be better than that which cost but twenty pounds if he has any skill that purchased it. Repentance cost very dear. Ay, it is dearer than if Adam had stood in the state of innocence to this day, and all His seed with him. It cost no less price than the blessed blood of the Son of God. The Lord in His blessed wisdom foresaw this, for it is not without His providence that our Lord would suffer man to drown himself in the debt of sin, that he might get a royal and kingly cautioner to relieve him of his debt. He would suffer him to be under the hazard of hell that he might get a lovely Redeemer. He would suffer him to be sin-sick for that end, that he might get a drink of the blood of the Son of God. He would suffer him to do that which procured him to be shot out of Paradise, and from the trees of the garden, that he might have right to the Tree of Life that grows in the midst of the Paradise of God, that bears twelve manner of fruits every month, and to the River of the water of life. And that certainly is better than his first estate was.

The Fathers said to this purpose, that the fall of Adam it was *felix culpa (a happy sin),* not that it was happy in itself, but happy in regard to the consequents of it; to have such a disease as will have the Lord of life Himself to come from heaven for the curing thereof, and take our sickness and infirmities upon Him in our nature, and make us partakers of His Divine nature, and clothe us with the robe of His righteousness!

And if ye will look unto us also, this is better to sin and repent of sin, than to live in a Pharisaical righteousness, than we had stood in our first estate; for there is no man who has such experimental knowledge of the goodness of God as that man has who has been over head and ears in sin. And our Lord gives not a fairer commendation to any as that woman, who washed Christ's feet with her tears, and wiped them with the hairs of her head. Christ says she loved much because much was forgiven her, for He had cast seven devils out of her (Rutherford evidently held the opinion, now generally rejected, that the woman who was a sinner and Mary Magdalene were the same person.) And Paul was a blasphemer, a persecutor of the Church, thirsting for the blood of the saints, an injurious person, yet being forgiven, and the Lord taking him into His service, he does more glorious works than all the rest of the apostles did. Now this teaches us two things shortly.

First: That we beware of turning the grace of God into wantonness. For whatever I have said of the excellence of repentance, and rising from the state of sin beyond standing in the first estate of Adam, and not sinning, comes all by accident of the grace of God, and no thanks to the sinner for it. And therefore let no man say because Jesus Christ is come into the world to die for sinners, and to purchase repentance and remission of sins, therefore we will live as we please, and go on in a course of sinning, for that is to tramp the blood of the covenant under foot. He who does so, whatever he be, he knows not the worth of the blood of the Son of God, and the excellence of Jesus our Lord. The dear blood of God that was shed for sin, should teach us to beware of sin, that seeing our sins put Him to such pain, shame, to so many sore scourges and wounds, and many sad hearts, put Him to those words, "My soul is exceeding sorrowful even unto the death;" "My God, My God, why hast Thou forsaken me," should not this make us to beware to commit sin?

And another thing this teaches us, is to let us see what our Lord will do unto them who come home to Him, that He will receive them graciously and pardon them, that no man may despair, and think their sin to be such that mercy and forgiveness and a welcome are above anything they can look for at the Lord's hand. If thou wilt come home to God and Christ, repenting for thy sins, and seek to be into the kingdom He has purchased, there is more remedy for thy disease than can be spoken of, there is more sweetness in our Lord than the sinner believes to be in Him. The coming to the kingdom, let be to the kingdom of glory, is like the Queen of Sheba's coming to see the glory and order of Solomon's court, she confessed she saw much more than was reported to her. If the natural man know Christ's welcome that He gives to a home-coming sinner, how He adorns, puts the robe of His righteousness on them to cover their nakedness, puts a ring on their finger to adorn them, and shoes upon their feet that they may walk the better in His ways, He gives them the joy of the Holy Ghost, and inward peace of conscience, gives them a feast of fat things, gives them to drink of the wines refined upon the lees; think you that they would love sin and the way thereof, as they do? Would they count so much of roses and lilies and *windlestraes* (stalks of grass) that will presently fade, and there is no more of them. No, certainly. It is because the world knows not what it is to meet with Christ, whose breath is heaven itself whose comforts transcend far the motions of all natural understanding, that they count so little of Him, and follow after other vanities. Oh, but there is much sweetness in meeting with Christ. Men know not what tranquillity and security under a pacified conscience are. Oh! but that is solid rejoicing under the hope of glory. Now for this hope's sake, and the hope of redemption laid up for the children of God, we render, to the Father of our Lord Jesus, and our Father, and to Jesus, and the Holy Spirit, all praise and glory for ever and ever. – Amen.

∞

THE WEEPING MARY AT THE SEPULCHRE

*"For as yet they knew not the scripture, that He must rise again
from the dead. Then the disciples went away again unto their own
home. But Mary stood without at the sepulchre weeping: and as
she wept, she stooped down, and looked into the sepulchre, and
seeth two angels in white sitting, the one at the head, and the
other at the feet, where the body of Jesus had lain. And they say
unto her, Woman, why weepest thou? She saith unto them, Because
they have taken away my Lord, and I know not where they have
laid Him." – John 20: 9-13*

In these passages of our Lord's Word, beloved in Him, we have
first set down the earthly witnesses that came to the grave to seek
our Lord after He was risen from the dead. And they be of two sorts.
The first sort of them are public men in a public charge, Peter and
John, the Lord's disciples; and how they sought Christ, and what
speed they came in seeking Him! The second sort of persons are
private persons coming to seek our Lord, Mary Magdalene, out of
whom He had before casten seven devils, And good reason that such
think much of our Lord, who have gotten renewed souls, or any
good thing from Him. Then we have the fruit that follows the apostles'
seeking of our Lord. They go their ways home again and find Him
not. Again you have the fruit of this woman's seeking of Him. She
will not give over her seeking Him, albeit she cannot find Him at the
first. Indeed it is a blessed thing for a poor soul to wait on still at
Christ's door till they get Him, albeit they should die there, waiting
for Him. And in her waiting for Him, first of all she meets with the
angels. And after she was comforted of them, telling her that He was
risen from the dead, and was rebuked of them for her weeping and
seeking Him there, she leaves them and goes on to seek Him. And
she meets with Christ Himself, and speaks to Him, but she *miskens*
(mistakes Him for another) Him as many times the children of God
are speaking to Him, and He is speaking to them again, and yet they
misken I Him. She supposes Him to be the gardener, and *speers*
(asks) if he had carried Him away, and where he had laid Him that
she might know where He was. And then our Lord discovers Himself

unto her by a short preaching that He made as our Lord. He is evermore *kent* (known) by His word, and when she hears Him speak she turns herself to Him, and she being willing to embrace Him she is forbidden to do it at that time. He would not have her to think so *meikle* (much) of her bodily presence at that time, because there is a better presence coming when He is ascended to His Father. Only she is commanded to tell the Lord's disciples of that which she had seen, and so she is made the first preacher of Christ's rising from the dead.

First: We observe one thing in the general that concerns the estate of our Kirk at this time. Herod and Pilate, and Jew and Gentile, they have all joined themselves together at this time to do the worst they can to Christ our Lord, and yet, when they have done all that they can, they cannot mend themselves. For now they had buried Him to hold Him down, and yet for all that that mends them not. The worst that the enemies of the Kirk can do to the Kirk is to put her to death, and yet when they think they have gotten that done, it will not do their turn when all is done. For wherever our Lord's bride be, albeit she were even in the grave, she *maun* (must) rise again, and in a triumph over her enemies. Let our Lord and His Kirk be where they will, He and His Kirk and cause, albeit they were dead, they maun live the third day again, as Christ Himself did, according to that triumphant and glorious word which He spake (Rev1: 17,18): "Fear not; I am the first and the last: I am He that liveth, and was dead; and, behold, I am alive for evermore." When John had seen His glory, and fell down dead because he was afraid thereof, He says that to him. There is news to comfort the Kirk of God, and to comfort all those who doubt whether our Lord will *tyne* (lose) the battle that He has against His enemies or not. No; He will make good that word that He speaks there of Himself: "I was dead, but I am alive; and, behold, I am alive for evermore." *Fra* (since) a dead man cannot do the turn, He will let it be seen that a living man can do it. We need not to doubt of it, but the enemies of Christ they thought that they were quit of Him now, that He would cumber them no more; but it is not so for all that yet, for He shall live when all is done, for all the ill they have done to Him. And within these few years our adversaries, they thought with themselves that long or now they should have been quit of our cumber, and that this gospel should have been clean borne down long or now. But with their leave Christ is letting us see this day that He will not have it to be so, that He will have that gospel which they thought to bear down so far, to come to some perfection again. So is the Kirk brought in, speaking in Hosea's prophecy (6: 2): "After two days thou wilt revive us again, and the third day we shall live." This gospel it *maun* (must) live, whoever they be who are against it, for the bearing down thereof, and the end of it maun be glory to Christ, and so those who are upon His side of it. Now, to say nothing of the race that Peter and John had in going to Christ's grave, it is said the other disciple he outran Peter, and came first to the sepulchre. John is he who is called the other disciple, and he outran Peter. As it is among the children of God, all of them have not a like speed. Some of them get a sight of Christ before others ever get a sight of Him. Christ has some into His Kirk that are old and experienced with His ways, and so they run fast in the same; and He has others also, who are His children and belong to Him, who are young ones, and cannot run so fast. But whoever they be who have the life of God in them, and so are walking on towards Him, they shall, either first or last, meet with Him without doubt.

He that came first went into the sepulchre and saw, and he believed. He might have believed that Christ was risen by that which he had heard, but he believed not till he saw. Many a time had the Lord said to them that the Son of Man must be delivered into the hands of sinners, and must suffer many things of them; that He must die and be buried, but the third day He shall rise again; but notwithstanding of all that He had said, John believed not till he had seen tokens that He had risen from the dead. However it be, yet this is sure, that it is good for everyone to use the means that God has appointed for attaining to the knowledge of anything. For John gat this *meikle* good by using the means at this time and coming to the grave - that he was assured that Christ was risen. Who was there eve that made a race for Christ but gat some good by their seeking after Him? Seek ye and ye shall find, knock and it shall be opened unto you. Zacchaeus, he had a longing desire to see Christ, and because he was low of stature, and the throng was great, he ran before the multitude, and clamb up upon a tree to see Him; and ye have heard what good come of that, as there comes *aye* (always) good of seeking Christ rightly: He says, "Come down, Zacchaeus, this day is salvation come to thy house." He will not fail, but He will make that word good, which He has spoken Himself, "Ask and ye shall receive, seek and ye shall find, knock and it shall be opened unto you." Could we be earnest in seeking our Lord - and I am sure ye know that this is a seeking time now, and never was there more need to be seeking at the hands of God - as the Lord lives, I durst promise it in His name, if we would seek Him we should see the salvation of the Lord. And so, albeit ill news should come unto us, let us not be discouraged for the same. But let us rest upon this, and put our confidence in the same, that our Lord is to be found of them who seek Him; and He has given signs thereof already unto us, and will do so hitherto if we will seek unto Him.

For as yet they know not the Scripture that He must rise again from the dead. The rest of the disciples, they believed not these Scriptures that foretold of Christ's resurrection from the dead. Can it be possible that there can be a scholar in Christ's school that has not learned his lesson that Christ taught him? Can it be that any who has heard Christ Himself make so many preachings of His resurrection, that they believe not for all that? Aye, ye may see the proof of it here. The doctrine that arises from this it is clear, that it is not the means, nor hearing Christ as a man preach out of His own mouth, that will do the turn to bring us in to God, and to make us understand things spiritual. Preaching, indeed, is God's means that He has appointed for that end, and the way that He ordains for bringing in souls to Him. But when all is done, it is not the only means of bringing us to Him. The special thing is that which is spoken by our Saviour Himself (John 3: 8), that wind that bloweth where it listeth, and no man knoweth whence it cometh or whither it goeth. We may preach unto you until our head *rive* (be rent) and our breasts burst; aye, we may preach unto you until doomsday, and yet that will not do the turn unless the inward calling of the Spirit be joined therewith. For an outward sound to the ear is one thing, and Christ's loosing all knots and removing all impediments another thing. Christ says Himself while He was in the flesh (John 6: 44), "No man can come unto Me unless the Father draw him." Christ is speaking in that place to them who had the outward means, and yet He says, it is no strange thing that they come not unto Him, albeit they have the means, because they want the Father's draught to draw them to Him. The scribes they heard Christ oft time preach, and yet for all that they consented to the slaying of the Lord of glory (1 Cor. 2: 8). Christ is preached there both to the Jew and to the Gentile, and yet for all that to the Jew He is a stumbling block, and to the Grecian the preaching of Christ is foolishness. We have meikle for us when the Lord's word is preached to pray to Him that He would join His Spirit and His wind with His word. Ay, all means that can be used by ourselves or by others are nothing without that be joined. It is in vain for us to rise early and to lie down late, and to eat the bread of sorrow all the day, if the Lord give not the assistance of His Spirit to the means that we use.

And again, we may learn from this that arms of men are not the things that will save us, if so be that the Lord Himself watch not over the camp. God keeps evermore the issue and the event of all things into His own hand. And this serves to teach us not to trust in means of any sort whether it be inward or outward matters, we should not *lippen* (trust) in man, nor in weapons, nor any second causes whatsoever, but only in the Lord Himself, that is the only strength of His people. And so learn to overlook second causes when you look that way, and look no lower than heaven, to Him who sits there and guides and overrules all battles in the world and all things else, and will let it be seen in the end salvation, salvation, even His salvation to all them who trust in Him.

What *gars* (causes) that it is not said, "They believed not Christ," but they "believed not the Scriptures" concerning this point? For there is no part of Scripture so clear as the Lord Himself when He is preaching with His own blessed mouth concerning that article of the resurrection from the dead, albeit it is true the five books of Moses and other Scriptures spake also of this article.

The reason of this is to teach us that Christ and the Scriptures they have but one tongue, and they who believe not the Scriptures they believe not Christ. It is not the sound of Christ's trumpet that many who profess to be preachers blow, but a sound from themselves and from men. This tells us what is Scripture and what is not Scripture.

That only is Scripture and no other that agrees with the will of the Son of God, and is according to His will revealed to us in His Word. And again, that is not Scripture, and so not to be believed or practised, which is not according to the Word of God. And so we may see that ceremonies and inventions of men they are but a dumb Bible, and a ground that none should follow for their salvation. If we have no other ground for our faith but only this, that the Pope, or the Kirk, has said such a thing, or the great learned doctors have said it, and therefore we believe it. As the poor men yonder over in the north, (Aberdeenshire was at that time the stronghold of Armenianism and Prelacy) they have been deceived by believing what grave-like men spake to them, and men who gat the name of learning. That is a blind guide to follow, and will lead us in the mire. But these that are indeed the called and the elect of God, they can discover the voice of Christ from the voice of men, and they only will follow Christ's voice, and will follow no other, whatever they be.

Then the disciples went away again unto their own home. They were over soon tired of seeking, for they might have waited on as well as the poor woman did. But God has our seeking of Christ, and all our supernatural works of that kind, into His own hand. We believe, pray, repent, seek after Christ and His Spirit, praise, hear, read aright, &c., as long as Christ holds us by the hand, but we do it no longer. A stone that is up into the air is out of its own element, and so long as it has an impediment it will stay there. But take away the impediment that holds the stone from the ground, *incontinent* (immediately) it falls to it again. Even so is it with us. When we are employed about these spiritual duties we are out of our natural element; and if the Lord take away His hand from the strongest of His children, a woman will go beyond them in doing good duties. Thank God for any good thing that thou hast, and that thou art kept in a good estate. They never *kent* (knew) Christ's help well who put man in such a tutor's hand as free-will, to be kept by it; who say that Christ has *conquershed* (acquired) salvation to all, and when He has conquershed it, He puts it in the hand of free-will to be disposed of as it pleases, to keep or not to keep it. This is to make Christ a fool merchant, and not to take account whether it be misspent or not; but Christ is not so. He knows what shall become of all whom He has bought. You know it is evermore the happiness of the weaker to depend upon the stronger. So it is the happiness of the poor soul to depend upon Christ and upon free grace. The happiness of the ship stands in that to have a good pilot; the happiness of the lost weak sheep depends on a good shepherd to seek it in again, and to keep it from the enemies thereof; the happiness of the weak, witless orphans depends in a good, wise tutor. Even so the happiness of lost and *tint* (perishing) souls depend on this, to *lippen* (trust) to Christ and His strength for their salvation, and not to such a changing tutor as their free will is.

But Mary stood without at the sepulchre weeping. Here is a strange thing to think on. The Lord's own disciples they ran away from seeking of Him. One of them that had said, "If all should forsake Thee, yet shall I never forsake Thee;" and yet here is a woman more forward, and more constant in seeking Christ nor he is, for all his fair profession. It is not fair words and a golden profession that will take a soul to heaven, and will make us to seek Christ rightly. We are all *meikle oblist* (much obliged or indebted) to saving grace in our seeking Christ. Here is a woman more forward in seeking Christ than all His eleven disciples are. Because she gat not her errand that she was seeking, she could not get Christ, and therefore she will not leave, nor give over, but will wait on and seek Him. A soul that is in love with Christ, they never get their errand till they get Christ Himself. Ye that are seeking Christ, never give over seeking till ye meet with Him, for they shall at last meet with Him who lie at His door, seeking, as this woman did, who say, "I shall lie still at Thy door, let me die there if Thou likest, and albeit it should come to that, I shall die, or I go away and meet not with Him." Ye may know the ardent desire of a soul after Christ can be satisfied with nothing but Himself.

We use to say the thing that one longs for is the thing they *maun* (must) have, and no other thing will satisfy them. A man that is hungry, and longing for meat, he maun have meat, and meat only, or else he is not satisfied, albeit he get some other thing. A man that is in prison and longs to be free, nothing will satisfy him but liberty. Even so it is with this woman at this time; albeit the disciples were with her, yet nothing can comfort her till she get her lovely Lord whom she was seeking. Learn that lesson of spiritual importunity, never to give over seeking of Christ when once ye have begun to it. Blessed are they that *ware* (spend in this manner) their time this way, in seeking Christ.

Mary stayed there weeping for want of Him, and yet looking into the grave to see if He were there. That is a good and blessed desire, and sorrow that is *backed* (seconded) with doing. That is heaven's sorrow indeed that is backed with doing and using the means. There are two things said of Jacob (Hosea 12: 4), that he wept and wrestled in prayer with God. What is the matter of a dumb sorrow for the want of Christ? But that is a right sorrow for want of Christ that is joined with using the means to get Him. As it is in Solomon's Song 3: 3, the spouse is wanting Christ there; she uses all means to get Him again. She goes to the watchmen, and says to them, "Watchmen, saw ye Him whom my soul loveth?" She goes round about the city, and to the daughters of Jerusalem, and charges them. That proves her sorrow to be a right sorrow for the want of Christ. And ye know what sort of tears the Scripture says Christ had (Heb. 5: 7). He shed tears while He was in His flesh, and withal He offered up prayers and strong cries to Him who was able to save Him, and was heard in that He feared. And that is the grief and sorrow that will only hold the feet when men are sorrowful for want of Christ, and withal use the means to get Him; and not only has a raw wish for Christ, and will not want a morning nor a night's sleep to meet with Him. That sorrow that is so is but a vain sorrow, and will do no good. What followed upon this?

She saw two angels in white sitting, the one at the head, the other at the feet, where the body of Jesus had lain. What needs this guard to be here now when the Lord is risen from the dead? They stay here to be witnesses of Christ's resurrection, and to preach the same to this woman and to the disciples. And Matthew, he has a circumstance of this preaching of the angels that John has not. "Why seek ye the living among the dead? "

Why are ye papists, to seek Christ at the holy grave now when He is risen? You may see that the work of man's redemption it is a very glorious and a very honourable work, for the angels in all the parts thereof are appointed to attend Christ and to wait. When He is born they *maun* (must) speak to Joseph and His mother to flee for His safety, they foretell His birth, when they are to return with Him again they tell them, and when He was in the garden the angels are appointed to wait upon Him, to *dight* (wipe) the bloody sweat off His face. And now, when He is in the grave, they are set to be a guard to His blessed and glorious body, and to preach of His resurrection. When He shall come again at the last day to judge the quick and the dead, He shall come with innumerable multitudes of angels - to let us see that the work of our salvation it is a very honourable work; and the angels they wait well upon it, and upon us. Even like a loving brother, who has his brother lying sick: O but he will run many errands for him in the time of his sickness, and will make all the house *ado* (astir) to get him well and at ease. Even so do the angels to us. They run many errands for us, and O but they are glad of our welfare; and (Hebrews 1: 10) it is said the angels are ministering spirits for the good of the heirs of salvation. Count ye little or meikle of your salvation as ye will, yet it is the angels' great task that they are employed about. They are appointed to wait on Christ, when is about the working thereof, both in His birth, in His agony, in His burial, in His ascending to heaven, and shall attend Him in His coming again to judge the quick and the dead. The Lord has them sent out to all the *airts* (parts) of the world to bring in His elect ones. Woe to ye who think little of salvation, since the Lord employs such honourable messengers about the same. Alas! the work of our salvation is little thought upon by many. Twenty - a hundred thoughts will come in men's heads from morn to night. And scarce have we one thought of this great work at any time. And what think ye shall become of them who are so careless of the work of the salvation of mankind whereof the angels are so careful?

These witnesses, they were clad in white. The angels, they have not our common country clothes, but they are like heaven in their apparel; to teach all those who are looking to be heirs of heaven to be clad like their country. The angels, they are clad with glory and with majesty, and therefore a sight of them will make a sinner to fall to the ground dead. If we think to be heirs of God in Christ, let us not be like the rest of the corrupt world. The apostle, he has a word for this (Rom.12: 2): "Be not conformed to the world, but be ye transformed in the spirit of your mind." When ye are drunkensome, and swearers, and break the Lord's day, as the rest of the world does, that proves you to be of the world, and not to have your affections up above. If ye would prove yourselves to be heirs of heaven, strive to be like your father, and like your country, and wear the livery of the house which is holiness: "Holiness becomes Thy house, O Lord." Mind the things that are above.

And they say unto her, Woman, why weepest thou? This would seem to be a needless question to propose to her, for she might have said, "I have *tint* (lost) my Saviour; who can blame me to weep? Who can reprove me for it, seeing I want my Lord?" But there is something in this question that is unseen, that is the reason wherefore they ask it, and this is it: "Your salvation is now finished, and the devils are casten out of you, and so what causes you to weep now? "Our Lord would tell us by this, that oft times we weep when we have cause to rejoice. She should have said, "This is the day which the Lord hath made, we will be glad and rejoice in it." "This is a day when a *decreet* (final sentence of a judge) is passed in heaven in your favours, that the lost seed of Adam is redeemed; and thou also art in the decree of redemption among the rest, therefore thou should not weep." O that we could learn to accommodate our affections, and all that is in us, to God; to weep when He weeps, and to rejoice 'when He rejoices. And when our Lord is without in the fields, it is not time for us then to laugh, and to rejoice, and to be feasting. It is a time matter for mourning, now when our Lord is out into the fields, and when His armies are out, and are in scarcity. And yet we trust that our Lord is keeping a day for us of this land, wherein we shall say, "This is the day that the Lord has made, let us be glad and rejoice in it."

Whom seekest thou? This question is *speered* (asked) at her to make her hunger to be the greater, for the greatest hunger that any has for Christ they may, always be more hungry for Him. And so learn to *rap* (quickly throw out) out all your desires and affections for Christ, not only love Him, but be sick of love for Him. That is more than ordinary love to be like to die for love of Him. And so all your desires and longing for Christ, strive to make them more, ay, till you come to that which the spouse has; "I charge you, O daughters of Jerusalem, if ye find my beloved, tell Him that I am sick of love. I charge you, as ye will answer to God, that ye tell Christ I am sick of love for want of Him," and till ye come to heaven to sing songs of Him eternally.

"*They have tane away my Lord, and I wat not where they have laid Him.*" This is her apology that she uses for justifying of herself in her weeping, "Why may not I weep, who once had Christ, and now I want Him?" That is a sorrow that may be avowed before God and before the world, to be sorrowful for the want of Christ. There are some who are sorrowful, and it is a shame to hear of it, the cause thereof not being good. Sorrow for want of my bairns, for want of my husband; sorrow for the loss of something of the world, or giving out something for Christ, &c; that is a shameful sorrow that cannot be avowed. But that is an honest sorrow that comes from the want of Christ. Look that ye *ware* (spend) all your affections that way as ye may avow them, and avow the cause of them before God and man. That is a sorrow that may be avowed that a soul has for want of Christ.

What is the matter and cause of her sorrow?

"*They have taken away my Lord, and I wat not where they have laid Him.*" He is out of my sight, and yet He is my Lord for all that; He is dead, and yet He is my Lord; for that she says, "They have taken Him away, and wat not where they have laid Him," is as meikle as if she doubted yet of His resurrection. And a little after she says to Christ Himself, supposing Him to be the gardener, "Sir, if thou hast borne Him away, tell me where thou hast laid Him, and I will take Him away." "I will think Him a sweet burden to come upon my back for all the pounds weight of spices that are about Him."

The doctrine is clear. To the children of God, *lost* Christ is *their* Christ when all is done. In Song of Solomon 5: the Lord's party, the Kirk of Christ, is there sleeping in her bed, and Christ, her husband, standing at the outside of the door knocking, and she says, "I slept, but my heart waked; it is the voice of my beloved." Thy beloved, and, yet for all that, He is out of thy sight. Let the believer's Christ be where He will, yet He is theirs. If they were in hell and He up in heaven, the believer will say, "He is my Christ, albeit Christ should cast me off, and not count me to be His, yet He is mine." So does

David's word as the type, and Christ's word as the antitype, testify, "My God, My God, why hast Thou forsaken Me?" He is a forsaking Lord, and yet He is their Lord when all is done. Ay, the believer will say, "He is my Lord, albeit He forsake me, and I will come to Him." Then true faith when it has the back at the wall will claim to Christ, and count Him to belong to them. And that is a very good mark of faith, that when one is setting Christ a *speering* (asking) on all *airts*, (quarters) and cannot get Him for no seeking, yet to count Him to be their Christ. This is the thing that the devil would fain be in hands with, to make you to doubt that He is your Christ or your Lord. This was the temptation wherewith he assaulted Christ our Lord. "If Thou be the Son of God, cast Thyself down from the pinnacle of the temple." All that the devil would be at in his temptations is to make us doubt that Christ is ours. But never give it over when all is done, but evermore take Christ for thine.

And, oh, that this land would believe this now, that He is our God, and the God of this land. Then suppose that our armies were put to the worst that are now out into the fields - as we trust in God it shall not be - but albeit it should be so, I say, yet seeing He is Scotland's Lord, if so be that we will wait upon Him, and trust in Him and in His salvation, it shall be found that it is not a vain thing to do so, but that He shall grant us His salvation who trust in Him. And to this Lord.

෴

THE WORTH AND EXCELLENCE OF THE GOSPEL

"For the weapons of our warfare are not carnal, but mighty
through God to the pulling down of strongholds; casting down
imaginations, and every high thing that exalteth itself against the
knowledge of God, and bringing into captivity every thought to the
obedience of Christ." II Corinthians 10: 4 -5.

The most part of the world, beloved in our Lord, there are but few of them who put that price upon the gospel of Christ that is meet to be put upon it, and so did some of these false apostles. They called the gospel foolishness, *daffing* (folly). They thought it to be but baseness itself. But men's thoughts are not the measure whereby this gospel is to be measured, for the Word of God and the gospel of Christ is not of the less worth in itself that men put a small price upon it. But our Lord He knows best what is the worth and excellence of this gospel of Christ. He who kens the vanity and daffing of the vain thoughts of the heart of man, He *kens* (knows) that albeit all the world should count light of His gospel, esteeming it but foolishness and daffing, and a weak thing; yet He knows that the weapons of that warfare are not carnal and fleshly, but mighty through the power of God to the pulling down of strongholds. I say nothing now of what I spake before, but only I say this:

Be no party in the world. Make the gospel and Christ your party, and take not the gospel for your enemy; for resist the gospel who will, and, whoever they be that stand out against it, it shall aye at last overmaster them, and *ding* (throw) them down, and tread them under foot, whether they will or no. How many have there been who have been setting their shoulders and their wits together to thrust this gospel out of the world. They thought it to be a cumbersome guest, and would fain have been quit of it, and so pressed to blow out Christ's candle. But they have been like drunken men, who in their drunken humour would run up to the top of a hill to blow out the light of the sun; but instead of blowing out the light thereof, they have only *kythed* (shown) their own foolishness. Even so do men in the world, climb up, upon the top of their worldly pomp and ambition, to blow out this candle of the gospel. But the more they blow at it to get it out, they only *kythe* (show) their witlessness the more. It has evermore proved itself to be master, and more, against all who oppose it.

A second *use* that we are to make of this, that the weapons of the gospel are mighty, is: Wherever this gospel cometh, whether it be to a congregation, to a nation, or to a particular person, it will evermore be master. We may not think to make a servant thereof, because it is mighty through the power of God. It is the arm of the Lord, as it is in Isaiah 53: 1; the prophet says there, "Who hath believed our report, or to whom hath the arm of the Lord been revealed?" And so never think to *bruike* (enjoy) the gospel and make a servant of it; for ye can no more make the gospel a servant to serve you than ye are able to break the Lord's arm. And, indeed, he is a strong party who will make the Lord's arm either to bow or to break. And, therefore, wherever the message of the gospel comes, let it have its own proper place; make it master. Let it prove to be the power of God to lay down those high and strong turrets of pride, of self-love, of worldly-mindedness, under the foot of Christ, that so He may be known thereby to be mighty. The gospel will not be a servant and drudge to any. It will not be a post-horse to run our errands for us. It will not be a servant to the greatest upon earth. If it be mighty, through the power of God it will keep its own place, who will, who will not.

Moreover, if the gospel be not the arm and power of God to bring us home to Christ and to salvation, it shall then be the blackest news that ever we heard in our time. It is not for nought that our Lord, who is mercy itself, pronounced such a woe against Chorazin and Bethsaida, even a more heavy woe than against Tyre and Sidon. Woe to you for evermore to whom Christ and the gospel come, and yet mend ye not. And He also pronounces a woe and a curse against these who bring not out the fruits of the gospel where it comes. And, therefore, it were best for you to bring out the fruits of the gospel *timeously* (early); for ye will not be quit of the gospel so easily and so lightly as ye *trow* (believe) to be quit of it. It will either mend you or end you. If it does no more, it will leave a summons at your door declaring that mercy and salvation were offered to you, and ye would not accept of it.

If ministers cannot be means to save people's souls, they will yet leave a summons at the door of your souls, and will take the sun, the moon, stars, the stones, and timber of the kirk, in witness that we did our duty, and told our Master's message to you, but ye would not obey. And, therefore, for Christ's sake, seeing the gospel is come to you, take heed that ye despise it not, as ye will be answerable to Him who is the Master thereof. In Revelation 14: 9&10 there is a woe and an everlasting curse pronounced against these who receive not the gospel when it is sent to them. And in II Thessalonians 1: 9&10, the apostle says the Lord will come in flaming fire and take vengeance on them that know not God and obey not the gospel of Christ. There is no less doom pronounced against those who are disobedient to the gospel of Christ, *nor* (than) the vengeance and the heavy curse of God. His word and gospel have not another word to say to the despiser of the gospel, *nor* the vengeance of Christ to light upon them. That is a heavy burden to light upon any. And therefore I beseech you, in God's name and in Christ's name, let the gospel have the one work, which is the proper work thereof. Let it be master, and think not to make a servant of it. Bow unto the gospel, least if ye bow not willingly unto it, it break you all in pieces.

Our weapons of our warfare, they have might and power from heaven and from God to *ding* (cast) down strongholds. Then it is so. It is but a *daft* (unwise) question and a foolish conceit of those who are enemies of the Lord's grace to say, that for all that might and power that is in the gospel, that yet, notwithstanding, the free-will of these to whom it is sent with that power, may say yes or no to it, take it, or reject the offer thereof, as your freewill pleases. This is nothing else but a conceit of those who never *kent* (knew) the power of the gospel. And we may know the gospel to be mighty through the power of God if we will look either to Him who is the author of this gospel, or if we will look to the matter that is contained in the gospel, or if we will look into the manner of the working thereof.

For the author of this gospel, it is no other but God Himself. Indeed, if this gospel, were the word of a man only, albeit it was spoken unto the soul of a man, then I think man's free will might say yes or no to it, as it pleased. But the gospel is not the word of man to man, but it is a love letter that is written to us by our Lord Himself, and is *dited* (dictated) by His Spirit. And why may it not command our will to yield unto it, seeing the Lord Himself is the author thereof? It is a great indignity offered to our Lord to say, Let Him speak as He will, albeit it were never so pithily; and let Him work with His word as He pleases, that yet, notwithstanding, to say yes or no, to accept or not accept as He pleases, that albeit our Lord shoot His arrows at man, yet He may either resist or *jouk* (evade) and let the fire go by him. He that framed the arrow He has put might and power in it, He has put steel in the point thereof that it may pierce where it lights. And, when He intends to bring in a soul to Himself, He shoots not as it were at the rivers and so to shoot at it *begess* (at random, by guess), but He shoots as it were at a mark; and He aims and sets right on before He shoots, and so cannot but light into the mark, and His arrow it will pierce where it lights.

Again, if we will look unto the matter that is contained in the gospel, we will see that it is mighty through the power of God, for all the world cannot frame and make up such logic as is contained in the gospel. All the wits in the world cannot pen such a glorious description of the New Jerusalem as is contained in the two last chapters of the Revelation. Nor can all the wits of men and angels make such a description of the Son as there is made of Him (Hebrews 1). All the world cannot come out with such a description of the power of the gospel as that which is here. And, therefore, albeit hell and all the powers had said that the gospel shall not prevail, yet seeing He said that it shall prevail, they shall not be able to resist it, but it shall prove to be mighty through the power of God, who is the author thereof.

Third: if we will look unto the manner of the working of the gospel, we will also see it to be mighty to *ding* (throw) down all our strongholds. If God were not omnipotent, there might be some show for this to say that man's freewill might say aye or no to the gospel of Christ. But He who knows all the several parts and the turnings of the heart of man, shall not He know how to win in into it? How can He make any creature by His power but He *maun* (must) also know by His power how to move it as He thinks meet? He who when He backs His word with power can win into the heart where there are seven devils and speak to it, can He not win into any man's heart how backward soever it be? I am sure there was never a man who had more hurtful thoughts of the Son of man, Jesus Christ, than the

Apostle Paul had, for he *dought* (could) not endure to hear of His name, nor to hear of any who professed His name, but persecuted them all most cruelly. And yet our Lord, He did no more but speak a word or two to him; and with these same few words He spake to him, He cast him off his high horse whereupon he rode so triumphantly, and lays him *laigh* (low) down upon his back and under His feet. And whereas he was going of purpose to persecute the members of Jesus Christ, he says to Him, "Lord, what wilt Thou have me to do?" To hear our Lord casting down, at an instant, such a strong and cruel opposer of the gospel of Christ, and presently to make him say, "Lord, what wilt Thou have me to do?" that is a cast of the power of our Lord's right arm. And so they are but fools to say that nature, or freewill, or man's heart is able to decline from the *straik* (stroke) of God's Word when He resolves to work upon them by it.

Now Lord be thanked that it is so, that we are not able to resist it but that it is mighty and powerful to overcome us. There is a *trim* (fine) place for proving of this point, Song of Solomon 2: where the spouse, which is the Kirk, is telling the manner of her well-beloved's working. He worketh by love. Now love, it cannot be ravished or hindered any way, albeit the lover may be ravished, or taken away, or kept away from the thing beloved; yet love cannot be so, for if it can be ravished or hindered, then it is not true love. In verse 4, "He brought me to the banqueting house, and his banner over me was love." And when the banner of love is holden up by Christ over the Kirk, is she able to resist then, and to hold Him out, as she pleases? No; for the next verse says when this banner of love was holden over her she fell a *sound* (into a swoon for love) (Authorized Version, " sick of love "), and therefore she says in the next verse, "Stay me with flagons, and comfort me with apples: for I am sick of love." This is our Lord's *gate* (way) of working upon the hearts of those whom He is minded to turn to Himself, He casts a lump of love over them, and when He does that, He can *gar* (cause) the rebel fall a *sound* of love (into a swoon from love). When a soul is running from God and from the consolations of His Spirit; when Jesus once sets His love upon you, and speaks to thy soul, it shall not be in thy power to resist, or to win out of His hand again. Let men make a principle of freewill, or determine whereupon it is that the word sets first. But when the Lord speaks to any, and backs His word with power, it makes them to set their heart upon Jesus; and the soul that Christ loves, He looks upon it in love, and, when the Lord does so, the soul is far from indifferent then, whether it receive Christ and His word or not; but there is a necessity laid upon them that they must yield.

And the Lord also, He is far from that, that He counts whether these to whom He speaks give obedience to Him or not. He speaks not so. But whoever they be to whom He speaks, if they submit not willingly He treads them under foot, and makes them pliable, and so makes good that word spoken, Deut. 30: 6; "And the Lord thy God will circumcise thy heart, and the heart of thy seed, to love the Lord thy God with all thine heart, and with all thy soul, that thou mayest live." Acknowledge your rebellion to God all of you, not only with that natural power of resisting the grace of God, but take with that wickedness and *sweirness* (unwillingness) that is in the soul, and that opposition that nature makes to Christ till He subdue it by His power. And Ezekiel 36: 26, where a new heart is promised by the Lord, and He promises to take away the old and stony heart.

But say they there, "That new heart that is promised to us there, it is promised upon condition that we resist it not." But look to the text, and ye will see that it mentions no such thing as "I will give unto you a new heart if you oppose it not;" but the text says absolutely, "A new heart also will I give you, and a new spirit will I put within you: and I will take away the stony heart out of your flesh, and I will give you a heart of flesh. And I will put My Spirit within you, and cause you to walk in My statutes to do them." There our Lord meets with the wits of men and opposes Himself to all objections that they can make of this kind, while He promises to take away the stoniness of the old heart, and then to give a new heart also, and to cause those whom He takes in hand to walk in His statutes. This in effect is our Christ's gospel. Even the power and the mighty arm of God to bring in the rebel soul to Christ and to make it Christ's own captive, and to make all of us say, "I find there is more life and power in His word than ever I could have believed there was to bring me into grace whether I will or not."

And, in effect, who are those who oppose this power of the grace of God? And it has been very well observed by learned men, that there was never any who opposed themselves unto it, but those who *kent* (knew) nothing of the grace of God themselves. And thus the grace of God it revenges itself upon them. Because they resist and oppose the power of it they shall never get profit or benefit thereby. And, indeed, few - few whoever *kent* what the power of the grace of God meant - durst take upon them to be an Arminian, or to speak against the power of the grace of God; but if any know rightly the power of the grace of God, it were the way to make souls fall in love with it, and to make them loath to say anything against it.

Now if this word and weapons of our warfare be mighty through the power of God, pulling down strongholds and such, we have sweet *uses* arising unto us from this.

First: O! If we could get your hearts summoned to obey this, that ye would come in to Christ, and give over your hearts to Him to be wrought upon by His word. Alas! If any of you have a bairn that is unlettered, ye will send it to the school that it may learn there. Others, through feeling of disease on their bodies, will have recourse to the physicians. If a man have a weak and troubled estate he will have recourse to the lawyer, and will entrust his cause to him. And yet thou hast a rebellious soul, and yet thou wilt not give over that to Christ to take and order therewith, and to work upon all the powers thereof, and to change them by His word. If we could once win on this far, to let God's word work upon our hearts by our Lord's power, we would then find that we get a sweet *niffer* (exchange), we would get a new heart for an old heart, we would get new spirits for old spirits. O! but that is a sweet and a happy change. And there is no way for us to become new men and women, but only this, by renouncing ourselves over to the power of God's word to be wrought upon by it, and, if we be not new men and new women, it had been better for us that we had never lived. Woe is to that soul for evermore that has no more of Christ than nature gives unto it! We may get some learning by being at schools, wisdom may be acquired by pains, riches, &c., and the world may esteem of a man for these things; but yet, for all that, he is nothing else but Christ's painted tomb. For all these, he is all rotten and filthy within; for as beautiful like as he looks without, yet within he is nothing else but the workhouse of the devil. Say of such a man what ye will, make him never so *trim* (fine) a man for natural parts, wanting a spiritual work, yet he is no other in Christ's account, but a *trim* limb of the devil. Will the world call him an *honest* (honourable or respectable) man, then he is an *honest* heir of Satan. If ye will call him a *civil* (outwardly correct) man, yet he is no other but a *civil* heir for hell, whatever the world thinks of him or himself. Yet this is the account that God has of a man so long as he has not given himself over to be wrought upon by the word of God.

Second *use*. If there be any here who are complaining of a rebellious heart, of a stony and hard heart, I say to such; "Look if ye cannot get faith to believe in this gospel of Christ, to lay hold upon these weapons that are mighty, through the power of God, to the pulling down of strongholds, and get faith to believe in it. Thou wilt not find the heart to be so backward. A soul which has such a hard, a rebellious, and a stony heart, it burdens them very sore. But here is a ground of comfort to such, if thou can get faith to believe it, that albeit thy heart were never so rebellious, hard, and stiff, yet there are weapons in Christ's armoury that are able to cast it down, to humble and soften it. Thou wilt say, "I cannot get my haughty heart humbled, nor can I get it win off the love of the world, and I find many lusts prevailing there wherewith I am greatly borne down." But here is our comfort, if we have faith to believe. This word of the gospel, it is mighty through the power of God to bring all these in subjection. If ye can get but this far as to be chased into Christ, by reason of the sight of your sins, it is sweet and comfortable.

O, but I like these souls well who are ever mourning for sin, who are complaining of a hard, rebellious, uncircumcised, stony heart. But here is a ground of comfort for such, that God's word is mighty through His power to bear down sin. If we could once win to this, to think that sin is a burden, it was good for us, it would drive us in to Christ. Thou art nearer to heaven when thou art bemoaning the estate of thy hard heart, and art putting it in Christ's hand to be healed, than when thou thinkest all well with you. Thou art meet then to receive of Christ's pity, for He is a Lord ready to forgive all such as come to Him in humility, He is a physician who will take sick folks in hand to heal them who have no money to give for their cure. He is indeed the poor man's physician. He seeks no more of us, but only to tell Him that we are sick. He has a hammer to beat down the hard heart. He has a sword to cut it in pieces. He can make whole the broken heart and afflicted spirit for sin; He can give a new heart and new spirit. Cast not down your heart, because ye find the hardness thereof; cast not away your confidence for all that, but believe in God's word, which is mighty through the power of God to bring it under these.

The Lord be thanked that there is this much power in the gospel of Christ, as to make a soul that is sick for sin whole again, as to make a hard heart a soft heart; that there is virtue into it, as to pour down that Spirit upon us, promised to the house of David (Zech. 12:10), the spirit of prayer and supplications, and the spirit of repentance and mourning for sin. And if we could attain to this, it were a sweet preparation for a solemn fast and humiliation when the Lord is frowning upon the land for the sins thereof, and the Lord is calling to solemn fasting and humiliation for the sins of the land; it were meet that everyone of us should take to heart our own sins and the sins of the land wherein we live, and be humbled before God for them, that so the Lord might comfort us.

Now, where are the fruits and effects of these weapons of our warfare? To pull down strongholds, to cast down imaginations and every high thing that exalteth itself against the knowledge of God in bringing in subjection, everything to the obedience of Christ. These be even all things that be either within or without a man that set themselves in any way against the gospel. It brings all of them in subjection. Especially it casts down all these fortifications that be inwardly in the soul against Christ and the gospel, even all these things that natural men trust to.

Now, whose is the house before this work be wrought? Matthew 12: 44, answers this question. Satan says, "I will return into my house whence I came out." So the good man of that old house is no other but the devil; and Christ our Saviour says in another place, "How can a man enter into a strong man's house, unless he first bind the strong man and cast him out?" He means there that Satan is master of every man's house until Christ come into the soul and bind him and cast him out, and take possession there Himself. That may cause all our feathers to fall, albeit so oft we will say that we love Christ. For *speer* (ask) at all men and women, they will say that they love Christ, and they are angry that any should think otherwise, yet by nature all of us are keeping a castle against Christ, and were keeping it for the devil's service. And of necessity before ever Christ come to dwell into the soul, all these high towers they must fall to the ground, and Christ must bring in a new work with Him, and make us new creatures, And this is one of the works of the gospel, even to lay all the heights that are in man's soul down even with the ground, to make sin and the devil and all these lusts that are keeping up the castle of the heart from him, fall flat to the ground together. And He sweeps all that muddy house to the door, that so He may make a pleasant house of ashler work for Himself. It seeks to cast down all the old rotten barns that formerly have been built there by sin and the devil, and to exalt us, that so the king of glory may come in as it is, Psalm 24: 7; "Exalt yourselves, ye gates; be ye lift up ye everlasting doors: that so the King of glory may come in."

All this serves greatly to cast down our proud natures, to let the natural and the civil man see in what estate he is in God's sight, albeit he have a good report before the world, that yet not withstanding he is not a man great in God's sight unless the gospel has gotten work in him to cast down the high towers that are in him. If thou hast never had a sick soul for sin it is a token that Christ and His word have never had any work in you; it is a token, if it be so, that as yet we are God's rebels; and woe is to them for evermore who are in that case, and will remain in it stubbornly. He has wisdom to call in rebels, and power to make them submit themselves to Him. But He has also a rod of iron to bruise them all to pieces, who proudly stand out against Him. Good it is for them who can give over the old house to Christ in time, who resolve that nature and their sins and their own old hearts will never take them to heaven. Aye, albeit they have some knowledge of God, and be acquainted with divinity that way liberally; yet they know that all these are no other but the keeping up of a castle against Christ, and building up forts against Him, and are made to acknowledge that we are ever in a woeful estate until the gospel comes in with the power thereof, and cast down all these strongholds that are in us; and to account so of ourselves that we know nothing till we know that Christ has thus wrought in us. Mark the speech of a learned man who doubtless had a very great measure of learning, yet he says of himself: "I know nothing, neither do I desire to know anything but the Cross of Christ and Him crucified; whereby I am crucified to the world, and the world is crucified to me." All the natural and *civil* (external good name) honesty in the world will not do the turn to bring us to heaven, till we once see that by nature we are in a damnable case, and, in God's mercy that if He please He may cast us away from Him for ever to hell. If we be not made Christ's captives we shall be captives and bondmen in hell forever. Except we become a fallen down building that Christ may build us up, we shall questionless be miserable forever. Now of this point a word or two of some things. First, concerning some ordinary faults that are in some, making them to hold by these towers. Next, we will show unto you some marks of these where these strongholds are casten down. Third, we will show unto you the way that the Lord keeps in casting down these strongholds.

Now for the ordinary faults that are in men in holding up these towers. They are:

First: And there is no man who is born without this: These walls of sin and strongholds they are not altogether casten down so long as we are living here. If it had not been so, one who was a chosen vessel of mercy, the Apostle Paul, had never used that speech spoken, Rom. 7: 18; "I know that in me, that is, in my flesh, dwelleth no good thing." This was spoken by him after his regeneration. And woe to them who acknowledge not that there is some of the old work of nature to the fore in them so long as they are here. Why? How can this be true? Because there is nothing that altogether expels original corruption that is in all of us but only glory. I know indeed that true grace lops away the branches off that tree, and wins in upon the stock also. And grace casts down the walls and the roof of this house. But for the root of this tree, and the ground stones of that house, there is nothing gets that *hoked up* (dug up) and takes order with it but only glory. Aye, the children of God, when the house has been chasten down by the grace of regeneration, they have been ready many times to build *toofalls* (small buildings adjoining a large one) for themselves again; as we read of Noah, Lot and David who fell in heinous sins after they were freely regenerated of God, and the falling into these heinous sins, was the building of *toofalls* and little houses of sin and corruption again.

But there be others again, against whom the Lord is shooting the arrows of His gospel, and yet there is not a hole made into their walls by them, nor a branch lopped off their tree for all that can be done to them. We may read of the like of these in Acts 7: 51, where the Apostle Stephen is preaching to some Jews, and in the end he says unto them: "Ye stiff necked and uncircumcised in heart." He shoots strongly at them, but there is not a hole made into their wall for all his shots, but they fortify it so strongly that it shoots back again at himself, who preached to them, and they presently stone him to death for what he did. And so did they to Christ Himself. He shot at them by the preaching of His word and working of miracles among them, to batter down their old walls; but they shot out again at Him and crucified Him. This is a pitiful mark where the gospel is preached to people, and it convinces them of sin, and all that that produces in them is that it raises hatred in their heart against the preachers of the gospel. But there is not one hole made in their old work for all that they can do, but it stands upright unshaken.

But there be a third sort of people whose old walls and strong towers, preachers, by their preaching, make to totter and shake, but immediately when they find their walls begin to shake, they set to to put props to them to hold them up; such as we read of Cain and of Ahab, they did this - they returned to their former pleasures and their old sins again, albeit their consciences were challenged for the wrongs they had done. And indeed, these persons are in a very miserable case, who get their sins discovered and laid open to them by the preaching of the word, and yet go home presently and away to the tavern, or, when they go out here, fall to their swearing, and so heap up their sins continually and harden their conscience. These are in a very fearful case if they were sensible of it.

But the best sort of the hearers of God's Word is those who bow themselves willingly to Christ our Lord, when He speaks to them by His Word and preachers, and are content that the Lord cast down their towers of pride, of worldly-mindedness, of filthiness, that He bring to the ground their high castles of self-love, lay under His feet their love to the world, cast down their conceit and love they have to superstition and idolatry. And in the Word of God, ye will find six several marks of such hearers as these, and we shall point at them. For the -

First mark, look at Acts 2: 37, where we have the Apostle Peter preaching to a number of souls who were converted to Christ. It is said, they were pricked at the heart by his preaching. The words he spake to them were such as if a serpent had stung them, they were so sharp they pierced the heart. When the Word of God begins to batter at the hearts of such, and to discover unto them the great towers of atheism that are in them, the high walls of profanity, the deep waters of bloodshed, the strong desires of filthiness, when they see such a slavery to all sorts of sin, and are borne down under the sense thereof, then the heart of the child of God it is stung, it is pricked, it is rent, and pierced, as it were by it.

The *second mark* of such is set down to us Jeremiah 31:18; "I have surely heard Ephraim bemoaning himself thus; Thou hast chastised me, and I was chastised." When once the soul is complaining of sin and is borne down under the sense thereof, and is sending up complaints both to God and to His servants against it, it is a token that these high towers are beginning to fall down, but as long as thou art continuing in thy guiltiness of sin, and are not complaining against it, that is not the gate to heaven. Albeit thou hope for heaven, yet it is not well with thee, it is a token that there are high towers into thy soul that the work of the old Adam is yet standing fast.

A *third mark* of these who bow willingly to Christ, and stoop to His Word, is this: They begin presently when their sins are discovered to them, to make syllogisms of their own, even as the unjust steward, who was shot out of his service, for faults committed by him. When he was out he begins to think with himself: "What shall I do now? I cannot beg for shame. None will pity me for work. I cannot work. And I have not of my own to keep me." And so he resolves he will go back to his master again. Let him cast him in prison if he will, for then he knows he must find him the means of living. Happy is the soul when it comes to such an estate as that; it sees it has nothing of its own to live upon, and so resolves it will go back to Christ. Let Him cast it in prison, if He will; it is in a better estate than it was then. Suchlike was the forlorn son when he had spent all that he had, and had no more. He resolves that he could not die for hunger in a far country, and, at the first, he thought he could not for shame go home to his father, yet when he saw that no other could be, he resolves that he will do it, go home, and offer his service to his father, for he thought it better to be a living servant than a dead son.

A *fourth mark* of these who stoop willingly to the gospel is: It raises into them an earnest desire after a Saviour. I will not say but in some this desire of a Saviour is not so thoroughly spiritual as it should be; yet there is some desire in him after Christ, and he sees that far, that he may not want Him, and he desires that Christ would come in into his soul and cast down all his haughty lusts and imaginations, and wishes that he were in body and soul made captive to Jesus.

A *fifth mark* of those who are obedient to the gospel of Christ is: He looks, evermore looks, to the promises with a long look of love. He never hears such a promise as that Christ Jesus came into the world to save penitent sinners, but he thinks with himself, "O! if I were one of these whom He is come to save. And O! if I could have my heart steeped into these gracious promises."

A *sixth mark* of those who yield unto the gospel is: There is no man who prizes Christ so highly as such a man does. O! he would give heaven, if he had it, to have Christ. There is nothing he would think too dear to be sure of Christ. You know that woman who is spoken of by the Evangelist Luke, who washed Christ's feet with her tears, and wiped them with the hairs of her head. If her hair had been heaven and her tears, she would have thought them not good enough to wash and to wipe Christ's feet; she had such a high estimation of Him. When once the soul comes to this pass; "O! miserable man that I am, who shall deliver me from this body of death," and knows how far thou art bound to Christ for delivering you from it, it will make you to put a high price upon Christ, and make you to say, "O! that I could give anything for Him that I might get Him. If heaven and earth were mine I would give them for Him." There will be no pinching then, when the soul is once truly humbled by the word of God. There will be no pinching then what we give for Christ. It would not be then, "Wilt thou give thy sinful lusts for Christ? Wilt thou quit thy pride for Him? Wilt thou quit the world and the things thereof for Christ?" We will stand upon nothing then, but we will quit all willingly that we may gain Christ. And these are very lively and clear marks of a downcast and humbled soul by the word of God.

Now for the way and order that the Lord keeps in casting down these strongholds. The text tells us that nature and the old man is first cast down, it is all shot to the ground; and so the law it has to work first to cast down before the gospel gets anything ado to raise up. And this is to let all of us see what estate we are in by nature, even in the state of damnation. I know this casting down of the old work it is rather a preparation for working than any proper work.

But what is the first work that the gospel works upon the soul? There is a question about this among some. Some say that repentance is the first work; others say that believing is the first work. But I think there can be no true repentance without some measure of faith preceding. But verily I think there is a work into the soul that goes before either faith or repentance. Our Saviour Christ has a word in John 6: 45, 46: "They shall be all taught of God. Every man therefore that hath heard and hath learned of the Father cometh unto Me." So there is a sort of hearkening to the word of the Father, that is in some before it be in others; and while He speaketh of a resurrection in the former verse, it is likely to be meant that that is the first work. Then this is the first work that is wrought into the soul - howbeit the habit of all the rest be wrought then also - even a spiritual hearing and apprehending of Christ by the soul; and then in the next place follows believing. And Christ our Lord He puts a difference between this hearing and faith, for the soul it can never come to Christ to believe in Him until it has once some apprehension of the first work wrought into the soul, until it learns to make a difference between Christ and other men by a spiritual hearing of God's word, till they learn to know His tongue to be a different tongue from all others. Where before they had but a light conceit of His word, now they esteem greatly of Him and of His word; and having attained to that, then follow believing in Christ and resting upon Him. And then follows the third work, a godly sorrow for sin, which indeed is formally the work of repentance, for whatever sorrow they had formerly, it was nothing else but a legal down casting for sin, but no true repentance and godly sorrow till then.

Use. Then there must be a humiliation and dowcasting in all who rightly know what Christ is. I would send all of you to this mark to see and try if ye have ever had this humiliation and downcasting, and consequently to try if ye have Christ. Alas! I believe I examine the most part, and ask them how they got Christ, and how He came to them, or when were their high castles cast down. I believe they must be forced to answer that they have either gotten Him in their cradle, while they were young, and knew not of it, or they have gotten Him sometime while they were sleeping; but for grief and sorrow for sin, for one tear for offending God, they never knew nothing of that kind. I would be loath now by saying this to bind sorrow for sin unto tears, for I know there is a true sorrow that is without tears, and I know there is a real sorrow that is beyond tears. But this far, I say, that there must be a true humiliation for sin one way or other before Christ comes into the soul. But alas! I believe all Jobs [Job 6: 4] be dead to have such sorrow, and find such grief for sin as he had. To have the arrows of the Almighty drinking up their spirits as he had, I believe the most part knew not what that means, as to have such a deep sort of offending at themselves for offending of such a good Lord, even, to be angry at the heart at themselves, for offending Him; and when this is, it will drink up the spirits.

I pray you try whether or no this work be in you, for many will be beguiled at the last day, thinking that they have gotten these things, and when it is tried it will be found to be nothing else but a plain imagination. And God, at the first, sees all such to be but false and counterfeit work; their repentance, their believing, and all that they have; and so that they are not in Christ. And therefore we should never rest until we get sure knowledge whether we be in Christ or not, if we be passed beyond nature as yet, if we be stepped from the kingdom of darkness to the kingdom of the Son of God. Lord, waken all of us to put ourselves to a trial in this point, and to see that we be not such who profess to be in Christ, and yet in the meantime remaining in nature. Now to this Lord, Father, Son, and Holy Spirit, be all praise and glory forever. Amen.

APPENDIX

༄

The Deathbed of Rutherford
by Harriet Stuart Menteath

༄

Tread lightly through the darkened room, for a sick man lieth there,
And, 'mid the dimness, only stirs the whispered breath of prayer;
As anxious hearts take watch by turns beside the lowly bed,
Where sleep the awful stillness wears - that soon must wrap the dead!

Hours hath he known of fevered pain - but now his rest is calm,
As though upon the spirit worn distilled some healing balm:
It may be that his dreaming ear wakes old accustomed words,
Or drinks once more the matin song of Anwoth's "blessed birds!"

Oh! green and fresh upon his soul those early haunts arise,
His kirk - his home - his wild wood walk - with all their memories
The very rushing of the burn, by which so oft he trod,
The while on eagle wings of faith his spirit met its God!

A smile hath brightened on his lips - a light around his brow.
Oh! surely, "words unspeakable" that dreamer listeth now.
And glories of the upper sky, his raptured senses steep,
Blent with the whispers of His love - who gives His loved ones sleep!

But hark! - a sound! - a tramp of horse! - a loud, harsh, wrangling din!
Oh! rudely on that dream of heaven this world hath broken in,
In vain affection's earnest plea - the intruders forward press,
And with a struggling spasm of pain, he wakes to consciousness!

Strange lights are streaming through the room - strange forms are round
his bed
Slowly his dazzled sense takes in, each shape and sound of dread:
"False traitor to thy country's law - and to thy sovereign lord,
I summon thee to meet thy doom, thou felon Rutherford!"

Feebly the sick man raised his hand - his hand so thin and pale,
And something in the hollow eye made that rude speaker quail:
"Man! thou hast sped thine errand well! - yet it is wasted breath,
Except the great ones of the earth can break my tryst with death.

"A few brief days -or briefer hours - and I am going home,
Unto mine own prepared place, where but few great ones come!
And to the judgment seat of Him, who sealed me with His seal
'Gainst evil tongues, and evil men, I make my last appeal!

"A traitor was His name on earth! a felon's doom His fate!
Thrice welcome were my Master's cup - but it hath come too late!
The summons of that mightiest King, to whom all kings must bow,
Is on me for an earlier day - is on me even now!

"I hear - I hear the chariot wheels, that bring my Saviour nigh,
For me He bears a golden crown - a harp of melody.
For me He opens wide His arms - He shows His wounded side,
Lord! 'tis my passport into life! - I live - for Thou hast died!"

They give his writings to the flames - they brand his grave with shame.
A hissing in the mouth of fools becomes his honoured name;
And darkness wraps a while the land, for which he prayed and strove,
But blessed in the Lord his death - and blest his rest above!

Others to follow in the Treasury Series include:

George Muller, Martin Luther, Robert Murray McCheyne, John Wesley, F. B. Meyer, C.T. Studd, and Hudson Taylor.

Other titles written / compiled by Stanley Barnes include:

All For Jesus – The Life of W P Nicholson

An Inspirational Treasury of D. L. Moody

God Makes A Path – A Devotional from the writings of
R. M. McCheyne

Sermons on John 3:16

Sermons on Isaiah 53

Sermons on Acts 16:30-31